THE HEATHER GARDEN

Heathers in an ideal setting in a New Forest garden

THE
HEATHER
GARDEN

Fred J. Chapple

LONDON
W. H. & L. COLLINGRIDGE LIMITED
TRANSATLANTIC ARTS INCORPORATED
NEW YORK

*Published in 1952
by W. H. & L. Collingridge Ltd
2-10 Tavistock Street, London, W.C.2
and in the United States of America
by Transatlantic Arts Incorporated
Forest Hills, New York
Half-tone process engraving by
Life Engraving Co. Ltd, London N.W.1
Printed and bound in Great Britain
by Fletcher & Son Limited
Castle Works, Norwich, and the
Leighton-Straker Bookbinding Co. Ltd
London N.W.10*

CONTENTS

ILLUSTRATIONS

7

LINE DRAWINGS

PREFACE

A BOOK devoted exclusively to the heather garden, covering most if not all the varieties of the various species at present under cultivation, is something new in current publications. I have felt that there is a need, if not a demand, for a work of this description from the number of people now growing heathers and kindred shrubs.

Lord Aberconway, President of the Royal Horticultural Society, in a contribution to *The Times Survey of Gardening in Britain*, puts his finger right on the spot. He writes: 'The big question remains—what are we going to grow in our gardens that gives us most pleasure for the least trouble? The answer, I think, is firstly and most emphatically shrubs.'

Since the end of the first World War heath growing has increased steadily; and it is hoped this book will be the means of stimulating further interest, so that the heather garden is assured of what it truly deserves—a permanent place.

And to others, without these picturesque evergreens because they have still to realise how valuable the plants are in many ways, there should be sufficient material in the following pages to encourage a start. Anyone with no experience of heather cultivation might well begin with about a dozen plants; many who have extended the heather garden beyond their original ideas began in this simple way. Even so small a number as twelve provides a show, which, I feel sure, will pleasantly surprise you.

A garden with a portion set apart for this purpose should not be regarded as a lofty ideal to be thought about in the future but as something attainable now, for if there is such a thing as a 'labour-saving garden' it might well be found where heathers have reached a stage of matured growth.

This leads me to a major problem of today—upkeep in relation to economic conditions. One need not dwell on such factors as labour shortage, wages, and the like, for most gardeners are fully aware of what it all means in the terms of hard cash. But I do say with assurance and in the light of experience that whatever the cost of the garden in a household budget the initial outlay on heathers is money well spent, a sound investment, rewarded by liberal dividends, not necessarily in cash but in the saving of time, labour, and work.

9

It is true we live in an age when material subjects are uppermost in the minds of men and women, who have become very practical in their way of thinking and mode of living. When it comes to problems of the garden, heathers provide an eminently practical solution.

I began to write this book in the warm melting sunshine of an autumn day. The heathers had faded except for the late flowering lilac-bell *Calluna vulgaris hyemalis*, a precious plant at the fall of the year. It would not be long before herbaceous life and many trees earned their winter rest; but not so the heaths, so far advanced in bud that *Erica carnea* Winter Beauty and Queen Mary would furnish us with fresh blooms before Christmas. The heather garden never sleeps.

Resistance of plant life to a prolonged hard winter depends to a degree on the previous summer. If it has been full of sunshine, the new wood is well ripened and the plants are thus renewed in energy. Early in the year following a sunny summer, the tree heaths and *E. mediterranea* are laden with buds, new wood is strong and well developed. Strengthened in this way, all the spring flowering heaths will resist without injury quite severe January and February frosts.

I write of the plants grown here for a quarter of a century; as they have responded to the influence of moorland air in a very exposed situation, nearly a thousand feet above sea level. With one or two minor exceptions, they are raised in open ground.

It has been my pleasure to visit other heather gardens where conditions differ considerably in warmer and more sheltered parts of the British Isles; but I found on the whole that most of the plants at such locations varied only in a slight degree from those of my own.

If here and there you find one or two salient factors repeated in the chapters, the intention is to emphasise their importance to those about to make a heather garden.

As it is my intention that this book shall be read mainly by gardeners I have used those names for garden varieties which are familiar to nurserymen and gardeners. These varietal names do not always agree with the botanical names as often the garden varieties are, in fact, clones selected from varieties occurring naturally.

To the living writers of the brief quotations which follow I tender my sincere thanks.

Whaley Bridge,   FRED J. CHAPPLE
  Derbyshire, 1950

CHAPTER I

THE HEATHER GARDEN

*Where room affords, the planning and
planting of a Heath Garden will give munificent reward*
THE WINTER GARDEN Stanley B. Whitehead

THERE are certain plants which disappear from human sight during the winter months and almost all deciduous shrubs lose their interest after the leaves have fallen. It is true that a herbaceous border presents a gay picture in June, but it is usually a pretty dull affair in the New Year. Now this is where the heaths and heathers score freely over their garden companions—they do not lose their identity or their individual charm throughout the whole year, even when the flowering period has long been over. The bright golden foliage of *E. Searlei aurea*, the faded russet-red bells of the Cornish heath, *E. vagans*, and the Corsican heath, *E. stricta*, infuse a warm and cheerful colour into the garden scene on the coldest and dullest of winter days, some months after flowering.

Just let us peep for a moment at a bright patch in relief to the background of our moorland country. Here we see the lively green shades of the hybrid *E. Williamsiana* whose foliage from October to March is as fresh as watercress in a clear running stream. As a winter study in contrast to the sombre upland, a whole bed of about 200 *Williamsiana* plants seems to have dropped from some distant Eden, reflecting the light and shade of beautiful colours, as though sunshine was always breaking into every little plant, and summertime, instead of being far away, seems to be very near. Then when the snows have melted and the ice is broken, the plants enjoy a new lease of life, glistening afresh and renewed in vigour, while frost, even up to forty degrees, causes them little injury. Thus we find the heaths and heathers at all seasons revealing the character of beautiful foliage—a feature quite independent of all their flowering virtues.

Twenty-five years' experience in the cultivation of these plants has provided a pastime which has never lost its fascination, quite apart from horticultural interest. Chosen as a hobby, it is in some measure detached from many familiar branches of garden technique; it is really an ideal sort of hobby as it grows upon one.

A man or woman may qualify as a heather fan without possessing the knowledge usually required for other garden craft, and no textbook is called for. Simplicity of cultural procedure belongs to the informal type of garden of which the heathers are a natural part; bedding-out like summer annuals is not in their sphere. It should not be imagined from these observations that this is a narrow or even a specialised side of gardening; the growing of heathers is altogether too simple for specialisation and calls only for moderate skill. They are easy fellows to cater for and nearly look after themselves, while anything in the nature of fussiness is foreign to their way of life. Few other plants require so little attention and repay one so liberally for the minimum of effort as their beauties unfold throughout the year.

The annual job of preparing, turning over ground, manuring, liming and forking is unnecessary, as the heathers do the work for you. They break up the soil more finely than anything man can do with a tool. Supposing you are dealing with entirely new ground and have taken off the top grass-clod: instead of following the usual practice of digging the soil you plant the whole plot with heathers. In three years' time the condition of the soil would be reduced to a fine tilth on the surface and a crumbling mass below that would give a stranger the impression that the plot has been invaded by an army of moles. It is, of course, advisable to dig the ground over roughly before planting on soil which has not been previously cultivated; but taking the heather garden as a whole there are no tiresome tasks to be done, and nothing that is really irksome as the work of planting proceeds from one easy stage to another.

Another important factor is labour saving and the gradual elimination of weeds. When the plants approach maturity and are close to each other much of the seed from weeds blown in the air does not reach the soil; even when some germinate the heathers quickly smother them. This is all to the benefit of the busy gardener in these days of labour shortage. (In one of the well-established heather plots here, 12 ft. by 9 ft., the average time in the year devoted to weeding is no more than ten minutes.)

It has been stated that heathers are suitable (and they certainly are) for rough banks and odd corners, to fill up gaps where nobody

seems to know what to plant. This is doing them an injustice, as
they are worthy of a better and brighter fate than relegation to
some backwater. To suggest an abandoned spot leads to a false idea
of their true value. They are for the open spaces of the garden,
where there is plenty of sunshine and wind, and all the light from
heaven to provide a rich harvest of flowers. Granted they can be,
and are, grown in the rough; but it is far better to make the heather
garden an attractive feature to be seen and enjoyed from a window
of the house.

Sloping ground with an undulating surface provides natural con-
tours for the plants; a grass bank with holes cut out of the grass
will do just as well; a flat bed with grass and weed removed is
sufficient for the job. They should be planted in groups, each about
18 inches apart,[1] the tall varieties being at the back or in the centre.
A plan of one of the writer's heather beds as reproduced on page
72 indicates some of the varieties to be chosen, the position of the
plants, and how they are grouped.

A long succession of flowering seasons is the heather garden's
way of bringing to the owner a perennial source of pleasure, and
the plants are, of course, evergreen. They never lose their charm,
not even during the darkest days of the year, when the beautiful
blossoms of the *carnea* heaths contribute so much sweetness and
colour. This extensive flowering period is found in no other class
of cultivated plant life; it is unique and exclusive to the heather
world, and surely it does not matter how large or small one's own
garden may be, the heathers should enjoy the space reserved for
them, being adaptable to most soils as sturdy, hardy, and vigorous
growing subjects. All they need is an occasional trimming with a
pair of scissors and clipping faded flower spikes after blooming,
although this job need not be done if found to be too tedious in
a large garden. Left alone in an open sunny position they will thrive
indefinitely.

Such then, broadly, is an introduction to the heather garden, and
the features lightly touched upon so far are subject to wider treatment in succeeding chapters.

[1] Eighteen inches may be regarded as the average distance, but the scale on page
84 gives more precise dimensions.

CHAPTER II

LAND OF THE LING

*Rejoice ... in the wiry spring of the heather and the harsh
grit of the rocks beneath your feet*

F. S. Smythe

BEFORE considering the private garden let us turn for a
while to the wider landscape which Nature provides over
mountain and moorland. I like the simple and brief name of
ling—a word pleasing to the ear as the plant is pleasing to the
eye. 'Take a sprig of ling', writes Ruskin, 'and you will find that
the richest piece of Gothic spire-architecture would be dull and
graceless beside the grouping of the floral masses in their various
life.' And I remember that Sir William Watson in his *Ode to May*
brings the moor and its wild life into four lines:

> *Where the pewit wheels and dips*
> *On heights of bracken and ling,*
> *And Earth, unto her leaflet tips,*
> *Tingles with the spring.*

Although limited to one species of its genus (*Calluna*) the many
varieties brought into cultivation have sprung from the common
form whose purple splendour appears unfailingly each autumn.
Many of these hybrids have been found somewhere on heather
ground, and botanical history, if we care to study it long enough,
may reveal to us how they came to differ from the common type.
Their creation is partly the work of the bees in cross-pollinating
plants, the seedlings of which bring out variations in height and
colour of foliage and flower.

Fond as we are of the cultivated forms in our garden we would
not care to be without the friendly ling of moorland origin whose
offspring display a few highlights unknown to their parents; here
a brighter and prettier purple, there a paler pink of more delicate
shade.

Gray tells us in his well-known Elegy that

> *Full many a flower is born to blush unseen*
> *And waste its sweetness on the desert air.*

14

These lines are appropriate to more than one beautiful heather which first saw the light of day in somewhat remote places e.g. J. H. Hamilton, a double flower of rich warm pink, was found in Yorkshire; W. G. Notley, a hybrid with all the fine delicacy of *Erica cinerea* and tiny, very deep pink flowers of the *Calluna* heather appeared on a Dorset moor; H. E. Beale is a child of the New Forest. Others are still being discovered somewhere by someone.

It is interesting to inquire how the ling of our common land is nourished to stimulate its growth, produce its flowers and perpetuate its life, as it has none of the advantages of garden soil. Peaty substances and accumulated, partly decayed matter are its food, apparently adequate enough to maintain the plant in a healthy condition.

But peat alone is hardly sufficient to keep ling alive, and if it were not for the moisture it retains and supplies to the plants, the blooms would not be as we see them after a hot, dry summer. Peat is the life-blood of common heather inasmuch as it is a reservoir at the roots.

At this stage, we take a leaf out of Nature's book and remember that heathers do not like dryness and, should the roots dry out completely, the plant is almost sure to perish. No amount of watering will bring it back to life. That is why on dry banks and in light sandy soil it is imperative to incorporate something which provides humus, leaf-mould, well-rotted parts of a compost heap (free from *recent* lime dressing), granulated peat, or some similar proprietary preparation that has absorbent qualities.

Moisture in the atmosphere is also valuable to these plants, which thrive on many parts of our western seaboard and on high ground where the rainfall is above the average of the country and there is humidity in the air. A heavy dew preceding a warm late-August day is worth a load of manure to the heathers flowering in our garden of the hills.

Fresh new life appears in the foliage of moorland ling in early summer and a luscious green sprouts from the undergrowth after the winter and spring rains. A. B. Austin's delightful book *In Your Stride* contains a chapter on June in which these lines appear: ' ... heather attracts no popular notice until it is purple, but who ever sang those waste places when the heather was as green as fresh grass?'

Who ever did? As the beauty of it is part of the sweetness of the year, there is no need to wait till the autumn for its splendour to mature.

Where ling lies in sheltered hollows it has a more luxuriant texture, softer and greener than on the moors; but the flowers of the latter are richer and deeper in colour, and the plants, though exposed to the rigours of hard winters, thrive with amazing hardiness. Take another leaf now out of Nature's book. Choose the most open part of the garden when planting your heathers; they revel in sunshine, wind, rain, and plenty of fresh air!

The low, matted, twiggy growth of ling is not due solely to the frugal diet upon which it exists. It is walked on by countless sheep and by human beings and the tip of the plant is a source of food supply to the grouse. Do cultivators follow nature in keeping their garden plants neat and compact? In a lane round the corner of our house ling has produced spikes seven to eight inches long, small flowers in a fresh pink shade. In digging up one or two plants they were found to be in no more than three inches of soil, mostly peat, lying on what seemed to be the face of a quarry: the spade kept hitting rock. How came those plants to be so sturdy, so attractive in flower on that sparse diet? The roots, not being able to penetrate beyond the stone (which was near the surface), spread out horizontally and were in a fine, healthy condition. After transplanting a few to the garden their lively growth was maintained for a while, but later they grew out of proportion to the size nature had decreed them and the long flower spikes were no more. The soil of the garden was too good for them, and much deeper than in their original quarters. In making far too much root, the quality of the flower suffered in consequence. I ought to have given them poor soil of little depth and added plenty of *their own peat*. This experience confirms what a retired Derbyshire man told me: that in the course of forty-five years, sheep farming he found common heather flowering at its best in poor soil of little depth where the roots were near the surface.

Another experience refers to an overgrown railway embankment where the line winds on its long climb through the hills to Buxton. After the area was set on fire plant life was no longer visible until, some two years later, the heathers reappeared, strong and bushy, hundreds of them, resembling a large collection of seedlings in a nursery bed. Each one was bushy from the root upwards and served as a model of how heathers should always be seen in our gardens.

Extensive informal borders of low-growing varieties flanked by tree heaths, and, in the background, brooms.

17

A naturalistic group consisting mainly of varieties of *Calluna vulgaris*, with the tree heath *E. australis* in the background.

A border of heather—the large flowering clumps are *Erica vagans* varieties, backed by *Daboëcia cantabrica* (left) and *E. arborea alpina* (left of centre).

HEATHER BURNING

It may seem strange to the reader that mountain and moorland heather has to be burnt and completely destroyed in order to perpetuate its life and provide renewed feeding stuff for sheep, lambs, deer and grouse. If the burning of heather were not carried out systematically there would be no regeneration. It is just as important to burn plants of a certain age as it is to produce fresh seedlings to replenish the crop, and only when firing has been done over a considerable area which is laid bare, is ground available for fresh growth.

Between the 31st of March and 1st of November in any year no person is authorised to burn heather without a licence issued by the Minister of Agriculture with prescribed conditions. The regulations preclude burning between the hours of sunset and sunrise, and there must be sufficient persons and equipment to control and regulate the burning during the entire period of the operation. Reasonable precautions are to be taken to prevent damage to adjacent land, plantations, heather, grass, crops, boundary fences, or to any person or thing on that land.

At least 48 hours' notice before commencing burning must be given to those who have interest in the land either as landlord or as tenant, and to any person in charge of land adjacent to that on which the burning is to take place. The notice in writing of intention to burn must state the date, time, place, and the extent of the area to be burned.

A forester working for the Forestry Commission over a Derbyshire game territory told me that he was not aware of any legal obligation for sheep farmers and gamekeepers to notify him when they intended to burn heather but they always informed him verbally a few days beforehand as a matter of courtesy. A Manx sheep farmer whom I met at Tholt-y-Will said in the course of an interesting chat that some farmers are under agreement with the Forestry Commission to burn the moor at regular intervals, for if it is left too long and the ground is very dry the conflagration may get out of hand and damage be done to surrounding woodland in which the Forestry Commission is interested.

No farmer burns the whole acreage during one season; he does it in sections, pegging his stakes to the farthest point of the portion under fire. This is not done to comply with any regulation nor in the interests of the Forestry Commission but to allow his sheep always to have heather upon which to feed.

Burning is worked in cycles, so that it takes seven years to cover the entire moor. In some parts the rotation is on a five-year plan. Extensive areas are burnt in Scotland in order to ensure an ample reserve of seedlings for new plants which should always be in excess of what the sheep can feed on. As sheep stocks in Scotland are so large, if the area burnt was limited to that in many parts of England 'the animals would congregate on the newly burnt ground densely enough to injure and retard new growth' (Dr Fraser Darling, *Natural History in the Highlands and Islands*).

Young heather no longer than nine inches is considered the best for burning, and after being fired in the autumn new seedlings—millions of green pin-heads—appear the following spring. It is another year before the plants become at all sizeable. These young plants are good fare for the sheep and their lambs. Old heather, tall and coarse, containing much hard wood, which is burnt, takes many years for young growth to reappear; if it is of a great age regeneration is improbable. On one Derbyshire moor it used to be the practice that where heather was burnt in the autumn no sheep were allowed on that ground between April and December of the following year. This enabled all young life to grow undisturbed by sheep. Birds will nest on burnt ground despite the absence of cover.

Dr Fraser Darling in his book, *Natural History in the Highlands and Islands*, writes: 'The food of grouse is varied, but the shoots of young heather are the mainstay of its diet. As sheep favour the same food the management of moors becomes the highest type of husbandry of uncultivated ground.'

Where there are large flocks of sheep the feeding on young heather is considerable, far more than is generally realised, and owing to the density of animal stock in some areas the growth of the plants is much retarded. The sporting fraternity has not always taken kindly to sheep on the moors, particularly where large numbers are to be found, because of the herbage denied to the grouse; but farmers have, in the past, resisted this opposition as they affirm that the value of heather to the sheep is in the winter time. When snow lies deep much of the varied herbage of other seasons of the year has died down and is no longer available as food for the sheep which turn instinctively to the heather ground where they scratch a way through and so obtain food.

This is one of the most remarkable examples of how animal life is sustained through prolonged periods of exposure on high ground where the temperature falls below zero—sustained on the simple diet of common heather. I have tramped many miles in snow over moorland country, facing an easterly blizzard, when often in places visibility has been reduced to a few yards—the compass being the only reliable means of finding direction—and, coming to a patch of heather ground, I have seen sheep taking both shelter and nourishment from the plants.

No sooner have the sheep trodden their way into the heather and scraped the snow from its branches than birds appear as if from nowhere to feed off the plants opened up by the sheep. A good crop of heather is the winter larder for wild life, as sheep and birds go instinctively together when nature calls them over mountain and moorland. If the sheep are removed from the moors then much of the bird life disappears also.

In the severe winter of 1947 the sheep on the Park Hall moor of Derbyshire were brought down from high ground and given hay which they refused to eat and no matter how much they were tempted they would touch nothing. This really was serious as it meant only one thing—starvation. It was then agreed to man a team to clear the snow off the nearest point of heather ground, tough work under arctic conditions—there was no time to be lost if the sheep were to be saved. When the animals returned to their native ground they immediately began feeding on the heather and were as happy as sandboys. Heather varies in height over many parts of the British Isles, and the long heather of a Scottish deer forest provides valuable shelter for the deer when snow lies deep in the winter.

What is considered by some men with long experience of moorland life as a better way of maintaining heather in a healthy condition with provision for ample growth of young shoots for animal feeding is known as Contract Cutting. A contract is arranged to cut heather on a patch of ground so many yards long and so many wide. The plants are cut down to ground level with a sickle and the cut branches tied in bundles and carried to the road where transport awaits them. The heather cut is used for thatching summer-houses and similar types of building.

Although the plants have been rather drastically pruned back, it is surprising to see what fine young growth emerges from the bottom afterwards.

In some parts of Derbyshire heather cutting is carried out as a regular occupation all the year round, excepting under bad winter conditions when snow makes transport difficult off the moor. A strong blade or scythe is used as the plants are mown pretty drastically. The cut heather is made up into two- to four-stone bundles, lifted by a hayfork on to a lorry, and delivered to firms who use it for packing sanitary pipes, steel and other finished products. These men work entirely on their own account and do nothing else by way of a livelihood. They are paid so much a ton by contract bargaining.

My main object in mentioning this rather unusual industry is to point out the wonderful improvement in the heather as it grows again after being cut in this way.

It may have something to do with breeding stock but most farmers assert that sheep are hardier on the tops—the higher the ground the sturdier they become. They feed on various herbs as well as heather. Lambs reared on mountain heather are said to be healthier and heavier than those brought up on lower green pasture. Why is this? One would have thought the food from the grass was better than anything the moor could offer and a sheltered valley warmer than the upland.

In the spring, usually about the month of May, lambs feed on new green heather shoots which have some nutritious properties to which the herbage on lower ground is not comparable.

It is apparent, then, that heather is available for much of the wild life of the moors when other food supplies fail, while it is recorded on the continent that the 'mutton of sheep fed on such pastures has a peculiarly rich flavour, and that the wool is produced in very large quantities'.

I have often noticed that sheep and grouse (as Dr Fraser Darling says in his book) make a good combination on a moor. 'The sheep not only crop the heather and keep growing the little green shoots of which the grouse are so fond, but they make narrow tracks which are bare of all herbage. Grouse use these, especially when the young ones are leaving the nest. They are able to keep the young birds dry when they move off for food and water.'

It is not an uncommon sight to see lame sheep on lowland ground where the pasture is grass which is not good for their feet. When the hoof becomes clogged for some length of time without any aid to remove the foreign matter foot rot sets in and the animal is not only lame but in pain. The hoofs have to be pared with a sharp knife. If this is not done they are sent up to the moors where their foot trouble is soon ended. Their feet are pared by contact with the heather ground, the sharp nature of the plants keeping the hoofs down, open and clean.

THE HEATHER BEETLE

As far as the cultivated garden is concerned there is little to fear from pests, to which the heaths and heathers are almost immune. My only enemy is the rabbit, who brings his family for an occasional outing into the heather world. On the whole little damage is done among so many plants and the rabbit is harmless provided he is reasonably clean.

But the common plant of the moorland has been attacked on a fairly wide scale by the heather beetle, *Lochmaca suturalis*. I have seen a wide area of heather in Derbyshire virtually wiped out and it was hard to believe that so much havoc had been caused by the beetle. The entire scene was completely desolate and altogether devoid of plant life; furthermore, there was nothing to indicate a revival of fresh stock.

Not only the beetles but the larvae feed on the young shoots of the heather, thus depriving the grouse of their natural food. The farmer who showed me his devastated ground was of the opinion that the beetle attacks the roots as well as the foliage of the plants, for some of the roots which had been examined clearly revealed signs of deterioration.

He went on to explain that the earliest symptom was a browned appearance of the leaves, assumed at first to be the effect of frost following a hard winter; actually it was the work of the beetle.

Mr J. H. Fabre in his *Wonder Book of Plant Life* says that the beetle is increasing, despite the efforts made in 'burning the affected heath, spraying with paraffin, dusting with naphthalene powder and other likely remedies to extirpate the enemy.' Disease among grouse which are commonly infested with parasites is partly caused by the lack of good food which the beetle has devoured. Black game, *Tetrao Tetrix*, appears to be the only enemy of the beetle, upon which it feeds greedily in parts of Scotland.

It seems to me that where suffocation is applied to beetles over a badly infected area, some of them escape to fresh territory, to breed again and cause more damage. Much of common heather, if cut down by a blade almost to ground level, will in time sprout afresh from the undergrowth. But the beetle must be doing more damage than merely eating the foliage; its activities apparently cause a kind of root-rot to set in.

COLLECTING COMMON HEATHER

There are certain types of people who wander about the country-side and cannot resist taking part of its wild life home with them. But when it comes to removing a whole plant with a stick or some crude bludgeon, or worse still, dragging it up by sheer brute force, much damage is done, as the plant will not stand for this rough treatment when in bloom—or when out of bloom, for that matter.

Sometimes I am told by very wise friends with all the solemnity of the human race that heathers will not grow in their gardens. Why? The answer is quite simple. 'We brought a plant all the way from Scotland (or it might be Wales) when we were on holiday and it died!' They express surprise at such misfortune and blame it on the plant.

The moral of all this is: never attempt to uproot heather plants when they are in flower. The best time of the year for transplanting is in the spring, and heathers of a fairly mature age should be left alone. I know it is hard to resist the temptation of digging up a fine big clump as you say to yourself: 'Ah, these are just what I want for my garden which will look like the moors when I've planted them.' It will not resemble the moors at all; most likely the plants will suffer so badly as to perish in the upheaval. Such plants are far too old for removing, the stems being hard and gnarled, the roots thickly tangled in stones and peat. To get them out properly would require a pickaxe.

The only suitable ones are seedlings, the smaller the better, and these are found abundantly in spring after part of a moor has been burnt. They should be lifted gently with a trowel or sharp knife, great care being taken not to damage the roots and so avoid injuring their fine hairs; leave as much peat as possible adhering to them. It is advisable also to collect a little peat (off the moor) in a basket or box or some other suitable container convenient for carrying, as heather collected from the wild to be brought under cultivation should at first be grown in its own soil, which contains the natural properties of acidity and bacterial life as well as moisture. To transplant a moorland heather from peaty ground into soil entirely different is a mistake.

Peat brought home in the basket is heaped into the hole and packed round the plant, and while the roots will in due course find a way into the soil of your own garden, by that time the plant is well established. Top dressings of peat may be added occasionally.

Just one note of warning: never plant moorland heather in good soil or in soil freely limed or enriched with manure. In good soil it soon becomes lanky and out of shape and altogether out of hand, thus losing its natural habit, while the flowers will be sparse and the foliage spindly. Better to plant in poor soil and add peat to it. For out of the poorest soil of the moors the best heather thrives and blooms magnificently.

This lesson from nature's landscape has been brought home to me during many years' cultivation of common heather in the most frugal mixture imaginable, in broken clay and stones—more stones, I should say, than the meagre quantity of soil—to which has been added well-saturated granulated peat. I remember at the outset seeing these young plants in perfect condition on their native hillside where the soil was so impoverished that it could hardly be described as soil. They never looked back after transplanting them in the way already described and they have never failed to flower as well as their parents did on the moor. The only attention they have had is clipping well back about every third spring.

From these observations it should be clear to the reader how essential it is for plants of this kind to be kept low in height and bushy, if they are to retain their natural characteristics of foliage and bloom. Grown in this simple way they will prosper indefinitely, flowering freely each year. The faded flower spikes should be removed early in the spring before new growth begins, and it is as well to remember there are no grouse and sheep to feed off the plants now in your garden.

The secret of successful cultivation of all heathers, whether of the moorland variety or any other kind, is to maintain a bushy habit.

What has been written here about peat and common heather does not necessarily apply to cultivated varieties, as the chapter on soil explains.

CHAPTER III

CHARACTERISTICS AND DISTRIBUTION

*From the middle of June the bell-heather or heath, begins to
emerge—its pale topaz bedecking the hollows of the moor.
But now the ling, too, is thrusting forth its bloom, the
smaller, brighter, and more beautiful ling. Soon the moors
will be a blazing stretch of purple beauty.*

Marriott Watson

CHARACTERISTICS

THE question is sometimes asked: what is the difference
between heath and heather?

Although to some people the plants seem alike after a
superficial inspection, there are distinct botanical variations between
one and the other, as, for example, in the corolla and the calyx. The
former is the predominating feature of the flower in the heath
(*Erica*), and the latter is the conspicuous part of the heather
(*Calluna vulgaris*).

It will be observed that the shape of the corolla varies from
globular to cylindrical, not unlike a tiny urn with minute teeth
protruding at the outer edge of the flower—this feature is characteristic in the variety of *E. carnea*, Springwood. Bright little stamens
emerge and the calyx is four-parted.

The linear leaves are arranged in whorls of three or four, sometimes as many as six; they are short and small-pointed. In *Calluna
vulgaris* the leaves are opposite and close to each other, in fours,
which gives a quadrangular shape to the densely-packed twig. Unlike the heaths, the calyx bears the colour and not the corolla, the
latter being only about half as long. The flowers appear in one-
sided racemes, some as short as an inch in length while others are
much longer. Colours of the heaths vary, but heather is a rose-pink,
which deepens during a long flowering season, and when in full
bloom over moorland ground appears to have all the richness of
purple in it.

There is no need to dwell on fine botanical points, except to say
that more detailed descriptions will be found in the chapter on
varieties.

26

Park Hall Moor, Derbyshire: a natural stand of heather.

A devastated area of moor, the work of the heather beetle.

Heather banks in a clough on Park Hall Moor.

A garden bank clothed with heathers, including varieties of *Erica vagans, cinerea* and *stricta*, with *E. carnea* for edging.

Above: Heel cuttings of various kinds of heath ready for trimming—rather larger than natural size.

Left: The leaves on the lower third of the cutting are carefully removed. *Right:* A panful of cuttings: they are inserted very close together in a mixture of sharp sand and fine peat.

DISTRIBUTION

The Ericas

The climate of the Cape, South Africa, is very different from that of the British Isles, and its comparatively mild winter enables the heath family to prosper luxuriously. Cape heaths are among the most beautiful in the world and there is one, *Erica Pageana*, which produces a yellow flower. As far as I am aware, it is the only yellow-flowered heath in cultivation.

Some of these, raised from seed under glass in our own country, are sold in large numbers as presents during the Christmas season. Rarely do they survive beyond the winter in which they were bought because of the frequent and often sudden temperature changes which are more than the plants can stand—from the greenhouse where they have been cultivated to the florists' markets, thence to the purchaser's home with its heated stuffy rooms becoming cold in the early hours.

That the Cape heaths cannot be grown out of doors all the year round in this country is lamentable—if only we had a South African winter there is no knowing what we would do with them!

Most of the ericas brought under cultivation in the British Isles are widely distributed over Europe, and those with native ground at high altitudes are generally hardy in England. *E. arborea*, which is found growing wild in the warm zones of the Mediterranean coast, will stand in our own country two or three severe frosts, but no more without sustaining almost irrecoverable injury. A prolonged hard winter will sometimes kill it outright.

On the other hand, *E. arborea alpina* is the hardiest of the tree heaths; it will stand forty degrees of frost. I have grown it for years as a very hardy shrub on high ground, and being a native of the mountains of Spain, over 4000 ft. above sea level, it enjoys our hilly country. I consider the flowers of *E. australis* the most beautiful of all the ericas cultivated in Britain, but the tree is not absolutely hardy like *E. arborea alpina*; coming from Spain and Portugal, one would not expect it to survive for long in temperatures at zero point. It is known as the Spanish heath; neither it nor *E. lusitanica* (syn. *E. codonodes*) the Portuguese heath, can be said to stand more than twenty degrees of frost. It is no use growing these trees, however attractive they may be in their own countries, if they are to suffer much damage in a bad winter, and successful cultivation is therefore somewhat restricted to the south-west of England and the Isle of Wight, where good specimens are to be found. I have seen perfectly hardy ones in the north-west corner of the Isle of Man.

More reliable is *E. stricta*, the Corsican heath, which withstands the average English winter remarkably well and I have not hesitated to grow it for many years. Although I place *stricta* on the border-line of hardiness, it only shows signs of being unhappy after long periods of frosts and a continual, intensely cold air stream from the north-east. It soon recovers in the spring, and I have yet to lose any of many plants grown in the open. As *stricta* flowers later in the year, the buds are not liable to injury by wintry weather. It is as well to remember that it hails from Corsica and Sardinia in a kinder climate than ours.

The house of Veitch produced a hybrid between *E. arborea* and *lusitanica* and named it *Veitchii*, which I have found to be as hardy as, if not hardier, than, the parent plants. My experience of the tree heaths (*stricta* and *scoparia* excepted) is that prevailing winter conditions, especially in the north of England, are responsible for so much damage to the buds as to spoil the bloom in the spring. It is for this reason, the injury to the trees during a few weeks preceding the flowering period, and not so far as general hardiness is concerned, that they should be grown only where they will do full justice to their beauty in the most favourable parts of the country, in winters milder than the Midlands and the north. There seems to be no object in cultivating plants throughout the year if the flower buds are to be blown off by arctic gales.

The name of *E. mediterranea* is rather misleading, as the plants, growing in southern France, Spain and Ireland, have no link with the Mediterranean area. How the variety *E. m. hibernica* came to Ireland is a matter of conjecture, as yet unsolved by botanical students. The mild, equable climate of western Ireland is conducive to their natural development, and the rain-washed seaboard of the Atlantic throughout the winter months, although bringing with it considerable damage by storm winds, is to be preferred to hard frosts and east winds in England. It seems feasible that migrating birds have brought seeds from the continent and seeds may also have come in shipping cargo. No evidence is available of collectors having introduced these plants to Ireland.

That the *mediterranea* heaths as a whole are hardier than the tree varieties there is no disputing; not one has been lost here even in the most severe winters. In 1947, for example, I had a fairly extensive collection planted out: *vars. superba, hibernica*, Brightness, *alba*, W. T. Rackliff, before the freezing air stream from Russia broke over them, and they had to face two months' severity, which was only part of the winter, unknown to heaths of this kind. Those prolonged blizzards had no equal, not even a parallel in all the winters of the present century, and the survival of the *mediterranea* plants was a miracle unprecedented in my experience. Most of them, especially Brightness, were seared round the edges by ten consecutive weeks of icy gales, but the remaining part of the plants withstood the onslaught.

Considerable damage was done to the tall *m. superba*, the somewhat brittle stems being broken by the avalanche of frozen snow which covered an entire plant about four feet high. All bloom was lost and the plant had to be trimmed back to about a foot in the spring. As there was only superficial injury at its base and the roots were immune from frost—or very hard frost—the plant made sufficient recovery to regain its normal appearance within two years. It grew again to a height of some four feet, and one could not help but admire its perfect condition, so fresh was the green foliage after the autumn rains, and the plant was smothered in bud.

In some parts of the country where there were frost pockets the *mediterranea* heaths succumbed that year; the frost was so severe that it killed the plants. This experience we were fortunately spared.

Another fairly tall heath, *E. scoparia*, the Besom heath, grows fairly extensively in central and west France and round Mentone in the Mediterranean; being the least attractive in appearance and flower probably accounts for its loss of favour in Britain. Far better known to our gardens are five indispensable species, *carnea*, the Alpine Forest heath, widely distributed over the central European Alps; *Tetralix*, the cross-leaved heath, found in moorland country in northern and north-west Europe; *ciliaris*, the Dorset heath, from the county which bears its name and also Cornwall and western Ireland—not a hundred per cent hardy (like *carnea*), but makes quick recovery in the spring; *vagans*, the Cornish heath, also seen in Ireland; and *cinerea*, the Bell heather, a plant familiar in many parts of the British Isles and elsewhere in Europe.

Added to these are *E. Mackayi*, of Spanish origin, and discovered in Ireland early in the last century, *multiflora*, native of southern

Europe; and *Daboëcia*, the St Dabeoc's heath, of Connemara, sometimes called the Irish bell heath, so closely related to the genus that it has now almost become part of it.

Descriptions of these plants will be found in the chapter on varieties.

Calluna vulgaris—Heather, ling

While the heath family of ericas is a large one, with several hundreds of species mainly natives of South Africa, there is only one species of *Calluna*. But what heather lacks in this respect it makes up for in many varieties, most of which are worthy of growing in our gardens.

For centuries the common form has covered vast tracts of mountain and moorland over Europe, and in the British Isles it has long brought pleasure to those who have seen it in bloom late in the summer and early autumn. It is described more fully in the chapter on The Land of the Ling.

As America has no native heaths or heathers, various species have been introduced, *E. arborea* as far back as 1658, *carnea* 1763, *terminalis (stricta)* 1765, *multiflora* 1731, *mediterranea* 1763, *scoparia* 1770, and *ciliaris* 1773.

To what extent the plants are now generally cultivated in the United States one cannot say, but heather (*Calluna vulgaris*) is naturalised in N.E. America, and grows in the South Atlantic States where the rainfall is anything from fifty to sixty inches each year.

CHAPTER IV

CHOICE HEATHERS

Through the sunny garden,
The humming bees are still
The fir climbs the heather,
The heather climbs the hill.

Mary E. Coleridge

I T would be asking for something too precise to name the date when heathers were first brought under cultivation. The past eighty years have borne good harvest in new varieties introduced by plant collectors, in improved forms which nurserymen have established, and in seedlings of unusual character. We should feel grateful to an enthusiastic band of heather hunters—H. E. Beale, J. H. Hamilton, C. W. Nix, Ronald Gray, W. G. Notley and others, who have discovered choice plants to which their names have been applied. Other varietal names refer to places, such as County Wicklow, Ireland, Mullion, Cornwall, and Darley Dale, Derbyshire.

One of the oldest varieties is still one of the best and holds its own against all newcomers. It is *Alportii*, a bush of erect habit with sage-green foliage and rich crimson flowers fading imperceptibly into a russet shade during the winter. Fifty summers must have gone by since *Alportii* first came into our gardens, for its name is to be found in old books, including earlier editions of William Robinson's *English Flower Garden*.

A modern companion to *Alportii* is C. W. Nix, which is distinguished from the older plant by its tall, graceful, feathery stems and flowers not quite as deep in colour but brighter. Both are very striking when their long and plentiful sprays are seen in drifts. They are valuable also as cut blooms, the slowly fading colour receding into a heliotrope shade, and when they are mixed with the golden foliage of *Searlei aurea* the combination is all the more charming.

A notable contribution to the heather garden in recent years is H. E. Beale, a plant of outstanding merit, the sprays not less than a foot in length (in some matured plants they are fourteen to fifteen inches long) being thickly clustered with silvery-pink rosettes of double flowers of exceptional beauty. J. H. Hamilton, County Wicklow, and Mullion are dwarf, the first a warm pink and, like County Wicklow, a double flower. The plant with the Irish name, of semi-prostrate habit, produces an immense number of shell-pink blossoms and, in the writer's opinion, is one of the finest of all heathers. Considering its low, horizontal, hard twiggy growth, the bloom is prodigious, and just as Springwood White occupies a high place among the carnea heaths, so County Wicklow is right on top of the calluna heathers. Mullion is another low-growing plant, profuse in flower, the pink colour deepening before the bloom fades. Although these double-flowering varieties have been extensively grown since they were first brought out, one should not forget a much older favourite, *flore pleno*, the first of the double lings to be cultivated. It has done yeoman service here and one specimen, fifteen years old, is more like a bush than a plant, sending forth spikes of soft pink flowers.

One advantage of growing heathers will be found in the long flowering seasons, from July to the year's end. There are actually two seasons, summer and autumn; *hibernica* and *hyemalis* belong to the late autumn period, the former being in full bloom in October, the latter in November. Visitors are surprised to see in mid-November a heather in full bloom, and on Christmas Day *hyemalis* and the carnea heath, Winter Beauty, in flower together. *Hyemalis* does not fade until the New Year, which is exceptionally late for the heather family.

Both are on the dwarf side, being neat and compact. *Hibernica* is smothered with lilac flowers; *hyemalis*, with more delicate tracery in the bells, is a paler shade. How picturesque they look and how well they brighten the garden scene at the fall of the year.

Of the many whites *Searlei alba* and *S. aurea* have still to be challenged, and even though Mair's Variety is taller in size and longer in sprays it is not so attractive a plant. The foliage of *Searlei alba* is quite different from that of any other heather, as its fine feathery branches of emerald green are so perfectly shaped as to resemble miniature conifers. In the *aurea* variety the luminous golden leaves are a foil to the other of emerald shade and a fully grown specimen is as handsome as anything the garden can show in midwinter. Even if they never flowered these plants would be well worth cultivating for the distinctive character of their foliage at all times.

There is perhaps no better white than Mair's Variety; its clear, blanched bell can easily be distinguished, and, being shaped to perfect symmetry, it is in a class apart as a rapid-growing, vigorous, sturdy heather. The clear white is not maintained for long, the blooms fading quicker than *pyramidalis*, and for this reason it has to be cut by nurserymen for the florists' markets as soon as the bloom is at its best.

Carlton, which should be seen in every heather garden, appears to have the largest number of flowers among the whites; in addition to the well-packed sprays of medium height, the laterals also produce flowers and so dense is the bloom that the leaves are partially hidden.

The only double variety in the whites, *alba plena*, has the reputation of being a classic plant, and many years' cultivation on the writer's part testify to the full recognition of this splendid heather. It should be planted deeply to enable the lower green foliage to bush out, and in this way its compactness is complete and strong growth is maintained. The spikes are fairly limited in number, compared with other whites, but each one is well clustered with large flowers. In my opinion—and I am open to correction—*alba plena* is the largest of the double flowers in the callunas. A wet summer suits it well, though many plants (particularly in the north) are spoiled by incessant rain and torrential storms; in such conditions *alba plena* flowers better than ever and triumphs where others fall below standard. But in a dry summer it is by no means as good. Another feature of the plant is that it is the easiest to propagate by layering. If I were offered only half-a-dozen heaths and heathers to grow in a tiny garden *alba plena* would be among them—it is absolutely indispensable.

Nor must one forget in the whites *Hammondii*, which has long given us unfailing service, and in face of all rival introductions we could not do without it. Choosing *Hammondii aurea* in preference to the type, we find that late in the autumn the tips of the stems begin to show as golden pin-heads, which the plant retains throughout the winter, and when it reaches the summit of new growth in the spring the fresh foliage of bronze-gold presents a gay picture. Friends have sometimes said to me while admiring the plant in this form in May: 'Are those the flowers?' *Hammondii* always displays robust growth and, like *Alportii* and Mair's Variety, quickly develops into sturdy plants; their flower spikes, plentiful and long, are excellent for cutting.

Torulosa enjoys high rank in the white heathers because it is the neatest and daintiest of them all, the small, bright green leaves mingling with exquisitely shaped flowers running prettily along the stem that tapers to a very fine point. This delicately poised, curling spray is exclusive to *torulosa*, giving it a finishing touch of an elegant character. How delightful it is in a rockery near the cinerea heath, *atrosanguinea*.

To the reader who is planning the heather garden let me add that no collection is complete without *tomentosa*, of Scottish origin— the white form which throws up magnificent tall white sprays and flowers on the laterals in August and September.

Two foliage plants *cuprea* and *aurea*, vary their shade according to season. The coppery hue of *cuprea* and the vivid golden leaves of *aurea* are prominent in the spring, but in the winter months both plants tone down to a reddish colour, displaying an unusual effect when seen in the fading light of a December afternoon. One is easily distinguished from the other, *cuprea* being more erect in habit, and *aurea* twirling loosely and irregularly in light golden stems. Both are rather sparse in purple bloom, but for some reason which one cannot explain *aurea* had more flowers last year than usual.

Another heather conspicuous by its foliage in the spring is *tricolorifolia* (Smith's Variety); the tips are coppery-pink and golden, the remaining part of the plant being green. Compact, with purple flowers late in the summer, it is a valuable new addition to the species—a seedling discovered at the Flash nursery of James Smith & Son, of Darley Dale, Derbyshire.

Tib, rosy-crimson, Mrs Ronald Gray, prostrate with reddish-purple flowers, and *elegantissima*, are plants of distinction. Ronald Gray and *elegantissima* have yet to prove complete hardiness with me. Several plants of the latter variety were in bloom one January when a sharp frost (ten degrees) came unexpectedly and killed the lot. I am inclined to the opinion that *elegantissima* should not be grown where keen New Year frosts are likely to occur; the sap is too high for so severe a check. I have seen perfect specimens of this plant in a more sheltered climate than ours, and in no other heath or heather were the spikes so long—twenty inches at least of soft lilac flowers.

The varieties described in this chapter and the remaining ones are included in chapter VIII.

A three-year old plant suitable for layering.

Fairly long side stems with plenty of foliage are pulled down and buried almost
horizontally.

Above: Layering of the plant shown on the previous page completed, with all but the tips covered with soil.

Left: The more usual method of layering is to place the plant in a trench, bending the basal part horizontal, and keeping it in place with a small stone.

Right: Heaths on a rockery. In the foreground are forms of *Calluna vulgaris Searlei* with an *Erica Tetralix* at right. In the centre are further varieties of *Calluna vulgaris;* at the top, mainly *Erica vagans* varieties.

Below: Formal beds containing one variety each, set off by conifers.

Hedges of *Erica vagans* in bloom. These plants are not trimmed.

CHAPTER V

SOIL

*Natives of the mountains and wind swept moors of Europe,
the hardy heaths are easy to accommodate in open positions in
most soils, so long as the latter are lime-free (the lovely winter
flowering species* Erica carnea *and its hybrid* E. Darleyensis
*being notable exceptions which tolerate lime), while the old
belief that peat was essential before success could be attained
has long been disproved. Experience, however, has shown that
all heaths do best in a freely drained medium to light loam, to
which may be added a little leaf mould, peat or spent hops at
the time of planting.*

From a Nursery Catalogue

Too many fallacies on this subject have been allowed to
spread into the mind of the average gardener; they have on
the whole done more harm than good and deterred many
from cultivating heathers. It has often been assumed and, unfortunately, taken too much for granted, that heathers require
special treatment, that they must have peat above everything else,
or that there should be no lime at all. There are some people who
still believe with all the good faith in the world that they will only
grow on the wild moors and that the white kind is to be found
nowhere else but Scotland. Whence came these unfounded ideas
no one seems to know and as they would appear to belong to the
realm of myth it is time such legends were exploded.

Perhaps it will help to restore the balance of practical thought by
making it clear that heathers will grow quite satisfactorily in:

1. Ordinary soil.
2. Medium loam.
3. Sandy-peaty soil (or peat worked into sandy soil).
4. Poor soil with peat added.
5. Lightly limed soil (see later notes).
6. An open situation.
7. Most suburban gardens.
8. Country gardens.

Avoid:

1. Rich soil.
2. Soil impregnated with lime (see later notes).
3. Fresh manure.
4. Artificial fertilisers.
5. Overhanging trees and shady positions (excepting carnea heaths).

It is better to plant in poor soil than rich. If it is poor, so much the better if you add plenty of granulated peat. Stiff clay, which heathers will not stand at any price, should be dug out to a depth of at least two feet and well-broken soil (preferably loam) substituted.

The soil where most of my heathers grow is medium loam, which breaks up well, crumbly to a depth of some fifteen inches; the subsoil consists of broken clay, sand and stones. It has not taken many years' cultivation to discover the value of these ingredients for the heath family as a whole, whether it be a tall tree such as *E. arborea alpina* or the small heather, *C. minima*. The humus of the loam provides sufficient food for the plants, the clay sufficient moisture, and the sand sufficient drainage. They seem to thrive more in this medium than any other I can think of, the texture of the loam always stimulating strong root action, especially when the plants have been put down for layering. During the abnormal dry period from Easter to Whitsun in 1949 over a thousand heaths and heathers of all kinds were transplanted as rooted layers in this soil and the losses were very few indeed.

Fibrous loam is undoubtedly an ideal mixture should you be fortunate enough to possess it, but it will be found that heathers grow and respond freely to the soil of the average garden, provided it is reasonably well drained, forked, and made into a friable condition—this tilth, as one would call it, is more important than all the soils put together.

As for peat, the granulated sort (peat-moss litter) is sold at a reasonable price and easily obtained in the convenient size of 1 cwt. bales. The bale is dry when delivered here by the local stores and left exposed to the weather in a pit in the garden for a few months before being used. Bought in the autumn, the peat is in excellent condition for the plants in the following spring and it goes a long way.

I do not recommend moorland peat, quite apart from the problem of transport. With the degree of acidity running pretty high, it is not safe to use straight from the moor to the plants, which may easily sicken and turn a yellow colour. I could obtain cartloads of peat from the country in which I live but I would probably find that most of it would never be used. After gathering it off the moor the peat is left in a dry shed for some time, until much of the water is drained away. Plenty of sand is mixed with this sort of peat before using it sparingly. Give me the loam any day.

Peat—the granulated kind—is usually applied as follows:

1. Heaped round the roots at the time of planting if the soil is on the dry side.
2. As a top dressing in the spring.
3. For cuttings of the Irish heath, *Daboëcia*.

The spring dressing imparts freshness and vigour to the plants—tones them up, so to speak, and improves the foliage. While peat used in this way is beneficial to heathers, it should be made clear that it is not essential to either their existence or their success; they will grow quite well without it.

A FEW WORDS ABOUT LIME

In garden books and nursery catalogues there still appears the stock phraseology that 'heathers should be grown in lime-free soil.' This hoary statement, which is completely out of date, has done more to prevent people from growing these plants than anything else. It is every bit as fatal to assume, on the contrary—as many, alas, have done—that peat is absolutely necessary to ensure successful cultivation.

When will these outworn theories disappear from common thought?

Because he has limed his plot at some time or other the gardener takes it for granted that henceforth no heather plant will grow in it. What an erroneous assumption! The truth of the matter is, after the soil has been sweetened by the influence of lime, it will be in better condition for receiving a colony of heathers. This may seem like heresy to some heather growers, who abhor the presence of lime, which is, after all, a matter of degree. If the soil by nature's provision is impregnated with it to the extent that no lime dressings are required, then it would be advisable to restrict the plants to the tree heaths, *carnea* varieties, *mediterranea*, *stricta* and the two hybrids, *Darleyensis* and George Rendall. While these heaths will prosper in calcareous soil, and probably *vagans* as well, the life of most of the others, particularly the Calluna heathers would be anything but a happy one.

There is, however, a wide difference between soil which is naturally of a calcareous nature and from which lime cannot be completely eradicated and soil of an entirely opposite character that receives an occasional dressing as one of many routine jobs in the garden. In the former soil certain heathers, most of them, in fact, are doubtful of surviving, in the latter they are almost sure to succeed. Just a note of caution: where lime has recently been applied planting should be deferred until the soil's condition is improved. Six months later or in the first year the tree heaths, *carnea*, *mediterranea*, and *stricta* may be safely planted; after two years *ciliaris* and *vagans*; after three years *cinerea* and Callunas.

One drawback in planting heathers is that many gardens have been so liberally dressed with lime over a period of years that the beds are full of it. In this case plenty of peat must be worked into the soil before planting ericaceous subjects.

In the drive for vegetables during the war about 10 cwt. of lime were scattered over roughly 300 square yards; three years later I planted two varieties of heather, *pyramidalis* and *minor*, as an experiment to see how they responded to the limed soil. Not only did the plants thrive as though there had been no lime at all but *minor* produced nearly a hundred healthy-looking seedlings. Since then I have not hesitated to plant all kinds and have risked as many as 1500 on that territory. The lime proved beneficial to the loamy soil and the plants were the better for it in the long run.

In some parts of the country the soil is of a light sandy nature, dry and often parched during the warm summer months. Plenty of peat (as previously described) should be worked into the sand, for most heathers grow splendidly when sand and peat are mixed. Throw copious quantities of peat into the hole at the time of planting, see that roots are saturated with it and don't spare the peat all round the plant—the sand will find its own way. Avoid trenching, as this will only bring more sand to the surface and so defeat the good work of the peat.

Another method, which was given to me a long time ago by an

experienced nurseryman, and which I have tried so successfully that I gladly pass it on to others, is to dig a fairly large hole, say two feet, and drop in the bottom a grass sod of substantial size upside down. Spread over the turf a little loose soil, and allow the roots of the heather you are planting to fall into the top mixture. If the soil is on the dry side water the sod first, and should peat be available (every heather gardener should have a moderate supply of peat handy for use in exceptionally dry weather) work it into the roots at the time of planting. The top layer of soil, not being of a rich nature, will maintain the plant in its natural habit during the early stages of its growth; later, the roots will thread their way into the rotting clod which provides fresh sources of food energy. Only with a limited number of plants can this method be adopted, as there would hardly be sufficient sods available for a fairly large garden.

The threading of the fine hairs of the roots into something which makes the operation an easy one is half the secret of successful heather cultivation, and as far as I have been able to make out there is nothing to equal loam, as it decomposes and breaks into fine soil. There are growers who add a little sand and leaf-mould (or peat) to pure loam, but I hardly think this is necesasary.

In soil which has been much enriched heathers grow on at too rapid a pace and there is a tendency for them to become drawn and 'leggy'. Although advice is given that they are best kept away from such substantial fare as manure, it is surprising the number of plants I have seen with this ungainly habit, as the result of acceleration in growth caused by over-feeding.

Such a condition may be partly remedied by clipping over the tops with the secateurs or scissors after the blooms have faded, preferably in the early spring for the summer-flowering heaths and in the early summer for the coming winter and spring ones.

I have referred elsewhere to a railway embankment which was set ablaze and the entire area denuded of all visible growth. The great colony of seedlings which appeared later out of that charred heap produced flowers more pink in shade than the purple common to the type; the spikes, too, were long and packed with bloom. A little heather world was reborn to the light of day out of very poor soil, peat and stones.

This is not to suggest that periodically one should 'fire' the old heaths of the garden in anticipation of a new and healthy family emerging at some future date (it is doubtful whether any would appear at all) but to provide a simple illustration from Nature's field of activity that special soil is not only unnecessary but altogether undesirable. All heaths and heathers should be kept neat and tidy, the Hammondiis and Searleis never being allowed to grow into gross, tall subjects as we sometimes find them.

Those who have long cultivated these plants may ponder awhile on what has been written here on the subject of soil—and I am quite prepared to receive criticism. What it really amounts to is that planting should be done according to common sense, and, without worrying unduly about the soil, the average gardener will probably find his heathers doing far better than he imagined at the outset. When they are seen flourishing in places he little dreams of, among gorse and bracken, over rough grass hummocks, and on dry banks, surely they will do equally well in his garden.

CHAPTER VI

PROPAGATING AND PLANTING

*Most of us begin our love of gardening at an early age,
generally with a tiny plot of ground and a few penny packets
of seed*
                                             Maud E. Stebbing

THE methods of propagating heathers vary among growers,
each one requiring a simple technique that is not beyond the
skill of the average keen amateur gardener. Modern professional nurserymen whose acreage is limited owing to high rents
and other economic problems raise their stock from tiny cuttings
dibbled into pots of sand and peat in tens of thousands, the pots
lying on stages in lofty, well-ventilated greenhouses or in frames,
some of which are electrically heated—although many are cold. This
may seem like mass production to some readers, perhaps in keeping
with the age in which we live; but whatever may be thought of it
as a form of commercial exploitation there is no doubt that excellent
plants are raised in this way. Two well-known firms believe that
the best heathers are those reared from cuttings; and as their
respective activities are working entirely independently and as far
apart as the south of England and Northern Ireland their judgement
must be respected.

My frank opinion is that the best methods are those most suited
to conditions of locality and soil, taking into consideration the space
available and the gardener's experience of general propagating
work. It is hardly advisable to be dogmatic in the matter by claim-
ing one's method as being superior to another's.

I have found that layering in open ground is a satisfactory way
of perpetuating the life of a heather, as the rooted layers remain
part of the parent plant until they are severed and are not raised
artificially under glass. Whether the young plants are as good as
those from cuttings is a question upon which opinion is divided.
My present stock of thirty thousand plants could be increased to
half a million in four years, rotating the layering twice within this
period; but I have neither the time nor the ground available to
proceed so far. An old-established Derbyshire nursery, whose

heather stock at the outbreak of the last war was in the region of a million, raise most of their plants on the layering principle, and as I have enjoyed many hours on their Flash ground in the pleasant company of a foreman who knew more about heathers and their cultivation than any other man I have met—now happily succeeded by one of his sons who worked with his father for years—I can testify to the sterling merit of plants raised by such methods. I have watched these two men on the job, studied their technique in putting down the plants, and twelve months later taking off the layers in beds prepared for them. All this is on a grand scale because they have acres of land upon which to work. The altitude of our hill-top country garden, with its pure air (like the nursery on the moors) has some influence on the way in which the life of the heather is renewed, and with such natural advantages at one's disposal, layering is the soundest way of propagating, while fiddling with minute cuttings would just be a waste of time.

But what suits me in my mountain fastness may be of little use to a man on the Essex marshes or a keen gardener at Weston-super-Mare; so I propose to describe four general methods of propagating heather—seeds, cuttings, layering and division—in order that the reader may choose the one which is best for his or her conditions.

FROM SEED

In a well-established heather garden seeds germinate naturally and I think the best and strongest plants are those which come from seed in the open. I have a bed of *C. Alportii* which has not been disturbed for years except for pruning well every other spring. The soil is not dug over and the only weed that appears is a creeping moss. Both in the moss and in the soil a steady crop of seedlings comes up annually and, being exposed, with miles of open country to the north and the east, they have withstood the worst winters since the outbreak of war. And yet for sturdiness only the *carnea* heaths rival them. Like many plants from seed, they are not all true to colour, some a much paler shade than the rich warm crimson which characterises *Alportii*. The bees are responsible for toning down the colour as they carry the pollen of *C. Searlei* and *C. Hammondii* (growing close by) to the *Alportii*.

Another happy hunting ground for seedlings is our rockery, for the seeds, instead of falling upon beds of soil, lie in the crevices of small stones on the surface—it is these dry chinks which prevent the seed from rotting. Not all varieties seed freely in this way; carneas and the mediterranean heath rarely do so with us, but the callunas germinate all over the place.

Heath and heather seeds collected from the garden are best sown in the spring. They should be stored in a dry box and kept in a shed (which should also be dry) during the winter months. Germination is more likely to be successful where the soil in the frame has come from the bed in which the plants were grown. Cover the seeds, thinly sown, with a little peat and sand.

If the seeds have been bought from a seed nursery, sow them thinly in the spring in a pot or pan consisting of well-drained sandy peat (one-third sand, two-thirds peat), mixed with rotted turf, the whole compost passed through a riddle so as to remove bits of grit and small stones. This will ensure very fine soil. After lightly covering the seeds with a little more fine soil, water liberally, place a sheet of glass on top of the pot, a strip of dark coloured paper over the glass, and remove the pot to a cold frame or greenhouse. The compost should be kept moist without being over-watered. When the seedlings are large enough following germination they are pricked out and planted in a cold frame. The soil of the frame should consist of sandy peat mixed with a little loam and made very firm, each seedling pressed into this compost about an inch apart. This is the way to establish a strong root as it fights its growing way into a ball of soil. Great care should be taken to see that the frame is ventilated, so that a current of air passes through it, the young plants kept well watered; there must be no forcing; and when the weather gets really warm the lights may be taken off. Twelve months later the seedlings are removed to a little nursery bed of their own, which is prepared in an open part of the garden, and, when large enough, transplanted to permanent quarters.

I once sowed some *vagans* seed in a large, deep box of sand and peat, mostly peat which came from boggy moorland heather ground. The box was slung right over the top of an open frame and left to the elements without glass protection. Two years later there was no sign of life; then came a very severe winter, with the temperature down to zero and the box of peat was frozen solid for ten to twelve weeks. Late in the next spring, scores of seedlings emerged, followed by more and more, until I could hardly believe what I saw, there were so many. I left them in the box until they flowered in the following year and there was a rich harvest of *vagans alba* and *v.* St Keverne. For a quarter of a century I have grown *vagans*, but none has been as sturdy as those which came out of the frozen peat box three years after sowing. To keep them separate from other stock, they were transferred to an open frame, growing so rapidly and making such powerful roots that I was compelled to move them again, for they were running into each other. In finally planting them in the garden they were layered at the same time, and I have now a collection of *vagans* heaths which have never been excelled among all others for magnificent growth.

This experience, which is unique, is digressing from the main subject of sowing seeds under glass. Rarely do they come true in colour, and there are more reliable ways of propagating.

CUTTINGS

The taking of cuttings is a rather tedious undertaking, calling for much time and patience and not a little 'green finger' skill which seems to come more easily to women than to men. I have watched women in a nursery (and working under glass in a municipal park during the war) dibbling their long and dainty fingers into pots of prepared compost, and have marvelled not only at the neatness of their performance but at the high speed of their work. The acid test of taking cuttings is, what is the percentage of the strike? One Cheshire nurseryman told me his was as high as 100 per cent.

Cuttings must be small, half an inch to one inch long, excepting the tree heaths up to three inches, of a soft unflowered portion of the plant. Half-ripe, green little things they are—no hard wood— taken in July or August, preferably July (September is too late).

A man engaged on the rockery in Kew gardens said to me: 'To many it is a sort of fetish to take cuttings in the autumn. Why should it always be September? Ever tried Spring for a change?' He went so far as to say that spring was a better time than late in the year. Although his advice came to me as something new, experience has proved over and over again that pieces of plants broken off accidentally will invariably root quite well after being pushed into the open ground and their own soil *during the growing season*.

The cutting should have the heel trimmed with a little of the old wood left on it and about one third of the leaves *carefully* removed from the base. It has sometimes been suggested the leaves be cut

away with a sharp knife, but I do not recommend th
heathers, as the knife can tear the bark of the cutt
damage after trimming the heel. I hold the cutting u
the right hand and gently take off the leaves with the
thumb of the left hand, leaving tiny pin-head ends on the
fringe of the cutting, like minute notches running a third of the
way, perhaps a little more, along the stem. A compost of roughly
equal proportions of sharp silver sand and granulated peat (passed
finely through a riddle) is now prepared for pots or pans or even
a small box. Some growers dispense with these altogether and take
the cuttings in a frame, using the same kind of compost. I remember
seeing a heather nurseryman putting hundreds of cuttings down
in the open, each one very close to the next, in sand and peat
pressed firmly to the ground in a reserved space at the back of his
nursery. He took them no later than July, kept them well watered,
and long before the frosts came the majority had rooted. His percentage of the strike was pretty high. During the winter months
the cuttings were covered with lights raised on stones. They looked
like a collection of green match stalks.

It is surprising how many cuttings one can dibble into a 12- or
14-inch pot or a large earthenware container. If the compost has
been thoroughly watered beforehand there is no need to plunge the
pot to the brim in water although it is usual to do so. The pots are
removed, after the water is drained off, to either a cold frame or
a greenhouse.

When the cuttings are taken in a frame or pots of cuttings removed to a frame it is usual to whiten the glass and close it down
for three weeks. The lights are then lifted slightly to let fresh air in.
Slight bottom heat will accelerate the rooting; electric soil-warming
may advantageously be used for this.

Not until the ground is warm in the spring and there is no danger
of frost recurring should the cuttings be carefully planted in a
nursery bed; it is important to keep them well watered in the
absence of rain. If the sun is unusually warm for the time of the
year, cover the cuttings with a little moist matter such as grass
mowings. When firmly established they should be transplanted to
permanent quarters.

Some cuttings strike much more easily than others; *Tetralix*,
cinerea, *ciliaris*, and *Daboëcia* lend themselves well to this treatment.
For my part, I waste no time with the paraphernalia of pots and pans

and silver sand and so on. I get a small wooden box, knock the bottom out of it, and place it on the soil of a frame. The box is half filled with granulated peat which has been in the open for many months, sometimes for over a year. A little gritty sand from an adjacent quarry or from the bed of a neighbouring brook is added. This rather rough and ready compost is pressed firm and the cuttings placed in it. A sheet of glass goes over the top and then a piece of paper; a stone is placed on the paper to prevent it from being blown away. Results have been satisfactory.

A large-sized crate, which once contained a consignment of pots, has been filled for over two years with granulated peat up to within three inches from the top. Scores of *Daboëcia* cuttings have rooted in it, as well as *stricta*, *Tetralix* and the hybrid *Williamsiana*. There has never been a grain of sand in the peat and only during frosty weather has an old coalhouse window frame covered part of it. There must always be some air circulating above the cuttings, otherwise they damp off after a change in temperature.

I like cuttings which have been broken off plants in the growing season; they nearly always root during the period of showery weather in April and the warmer days of May—the ground must be on the damp side when they are put in the soil where the parent plants grow.

LAYERING

The advantage of layering is to be found in its simplicity and its sure success. Layers are not severed at the outset from the main plant, as in the case of cuttings taken away for artificial treatment under glass, but all the while are making fibrous root, left undisturbed throughout the growing period and flowering as cheerfully as the parent plant itself of which they are a part. Side pieces of fairly long branches with *plenty of new foliage* are pulled down and placed almost horizontally into the soil. It is very important that the ends appear just *above* soil level as these are to make the new growth from the many green stems they contain.

If the entire length of the layer is buried it will probably rot during the winter months; in any case, one should not expect to find new growth from hard wood. Therefore it is essential that the end of the stem emerging above soil level be turned vertically towards the sky.

Where the bend occurs the flow of the sap is retarded, and at the acute elbow turn, root action is stimulated. If the branch laid down is not sufficiently turned, the sap flows normally to the tips and it might just as well have not been laid down at all—it is a mere waste of time, for rooting (if any) is very slow and of poor quality.

End portions full of fresh green leaves on plants no more than six years old root readily when turned upwards in the manner described; they soon increase in size, making bushy clumps from which a plentiful number of new plants will be obtained after the layers are cut. Should the lower branches be too high above the ground the plant may be lifted carefully with a spade and replanted a little deeper. Do not bury it.

There is no need to notch or peg the layers, but to avoid the stems springing back a moderate-sized stone or half a brick is placed on the soil about midway along the stem. This will keep the layer down in a rigid position and conserve moisture. If peat and sand fill the shallow trench containing the layer, root action is stimulated, but these ingredients are not essential as long as the soil is well broken up; in fact, *vagans* layers better and more quickly in crumbling loam than in peat compost.

Some soils are more naturally suited to provide rapid root action than others; in my garden I have seen the layers of *C. Searlei alba* and *vagans* St Keverne cut in about four months, the layers being put down at the end of April and cut at the beginning of September, with an assurance that the roots so far developed were strong enough to maintain the young plant after being removed from the parent.

The layering can be done at any time of the year excepting frosty or very bad weather. Spring is an ideal season for putting down the layers, which are usually left undisturbed for twelve months. After the young branches have been cut, they should be planted in fine loose soil. If they have made a fairly large clump, plant the clump as one complete whole instead of being tempted to divide into so many small plants. It is surprising how strong these clumps become and, after further growth, how well they divide twelve months later. These stronger divisions make far more plants than if division had been made a year previously. Always divide from the roots, which should be held in the hands and broken carefully. Never split the stems downwards as this can bring about much damage not only to the roots but to the plant itself.

In digging up a plant for layering, I do not always put it down again vertically. Some of the soil in which it was grown is removed and a trench made about as deep as the plant itself; in this the plant is placed, part horizontally, part vertically. The top foliage must appear just above ground level when the soil is thrown back, into the trench, to cover the plant.

The stems of the top foliage are spread out fanwise to allow plenty of air to pass through them and well-forked soil between them; the ends of the stems, the only portion of the plant now visible, is turned up skywards. It is as well to keep the surface soil hoed from time to time; this should be done lightly with the fingers, and not with a tool, the sharp edge of which would easily damage the tiny roots developing in the young stems.

Twelve months later when the plant is dug up again, so much growth has been established that the main stem can be cut below the layered part and the old, original root discarded. The clump is then planted afresh in friable soil and in another year's time becomes a mass of fibrous roots which will divide into quite a number of new plants. This is layering on a plan of two-years' rotation; in April for all varieties excepting *carnea* and *mediterranea*, which are propagated in May.

Another method of layering refers to old plants, but I think these are best left alone as far as general propagating is concerned. Accidentally I came across a *Searlei alba* hidden beneath an ever-extending escallonia shrub. The heather was sadly drawn and looked a pretty miserable specimen, with most of the branches denuded of foliage and only a little green life remained at the tips. Almost any gardener would have thrown it out.

I dug it up for experimental purposes, taking great care to lift the roots as one whole with the soil clinging to them. (When digging up a heather always put the spade well into the ground and lift the plant and its ball of soil as a solid mass. The wrong way is to disturb the root system by breaking the roots and leaving them in a distended condition; a heather so disrupted is much harder to transplant). I took the old Searlei on to ground (adjacent to the main garden) where most of the heathers grow, and made a hole two feet deep, and dropped the plant into it. Even a couple of feet was not enough, so more soil had to come out. With almost the whole of the plant buried the long bare branches were pulled away from their upright position and turned back horizontally until the green ends were just above soil level. These ends then formed a circle round the plant and in a shallow trench which was made in the circle I added some peat and sand. Each of the minute green ends was turned up skywards and when the soil was thrown back into the hole they were the only signs of life visible.

This was done in April; by the following September the ends had bushed out into fine big clumps; so robust was root action that they could have been cut in the autumn. But I left them until the coming spring, severed the clumps, a dozen and more, and planted them in open ground. Divisions of the clumps a year later produced about eighty very healthy plants. And all these from mere sprigs, like bits of parsley, off a decrepit old *Searlei!*

Although I mention this experiment as a matter of interest, I do not commend such methods to the average gardener, who probably has neither the time nor the space available for such work. It is, however, one of the ways of propagating rhododendrons.

Old plants (ten years and over) should not be uprooted and re-planted deeply to encourage (feeble) root development along the bare upright stems. This method is out of date. It only produces anaemic plants completely lacking in vitality. Plants so aged are better left where they are and cut down to a third of their size. This seems rather drastic, but I write from experience, knowing full well that no harm will come to them. Fresh growth from the base will soon improve their appearance and the flowers will be better and more plentiful.

I am not one to advocate digging up a heather and splitting it with a tool in order to make more. This is all right with herbaceous subjects, but the last thing one should do with a heather plant is to drive a spade through it; the damage thus caused is almost irreparable. Some plants root more quickly and more strongly than others; this applies particularly to the Calluna heathers *Hammondii*, *Searlei*, Mair's variety and *Alportii*. They can easily be divided with the hands within the first six years of the plant's life. On the other hand, one grown from a cutting and planted out on one 'leg' will never divide.

From the habit of these plants it seems more natural for the heathers to be propagated by layering, while many of the heaths— *cinerea*, *ciliaris* and *Tetralix*—are more adaptable for cuttings.

PLANTING

Plant deeply always, with the lowest portion of the foliage resting on the soil. The plant should appear as just 'sitting comfortable' on the ground. It is surprising how many gardeners fail to observe this elementary beginning of a young plant's life. It prevents the stems (of some plants) looking in the course of time like a network of bare wires from the base up to the green part. No long bare stems should be seen in a well-grown heather. If they are partly bare when they come from a nursery, bury the bare part in the soil either vertically or partly horizontally and bring the green to the ground level. Heathers look natural after being planted in this way.

There is no need to press the plants firmly as in the case of alpines, or tread the soil as in the case of shrubs. Instead of pressing them I work the soil fairly loosely round the plant, with a hand fork. "Working" the soil in this way is important, as heathers do not take kindly to lumpy or hard substances. A friable condition is what they enjoy.

TRIMMING

Friends new to heather cultivation ask me sometimes if pruning should be done; if so, at what time of the year? Pruning, which means the cutting back with shears or secateurs at regular intervals, is unnecessary in the heather garden. As long as the heaths are planted in the way I have described, all they need is an annual trimming with a sharp pair of scissors. The secateurs or shears will have to be used if the plants are fairly old and have received no attention for some years. Only the faded blooms should be cut from the plant, just before new growth begins to develop in early spring. I have already mentioned this in the chapter on the wild ling and it applies as well to all the cultivated varieties.

After clipping over the tops regularly it will be seen how well the plants maintain their neat, bushy shape, which was apparent, or should have been, when they were first planted. Left unattended indefinitely they are inclined to become ragged, and, in the course of time, rather ungainly, because that part of the main stem which covers the flowering portion is thinner and weaker. If these slender portions are allowed to remain after each successive year's flowering,

The double white form of *Calluna vulgaris, alba plena*

A well-grown plant of *Erica vagans alba.*

The neat rounded cushions of *Calluna vulgaris Foxii*.

With its long silvery-pink spikes, H. E. Beale is one of the choicest varieties of calluna.

Calluna County Wicklow has double, shell-pink flowers.

Tomentosa is one of the many white lings, and grows to about 18 ins. It is here shown in bud.

The white bells of *Daboëcia cantabrica var. alba,* growing on a rock garden.

The purple form of *Daboëcia cantabrica,* variety *atropurpurea.*

the plant loses a certain degree of vitality. The way to prevent them from appearing is to cut the blooms.

Once the blooms are removed, new growth has to start afresh from *below* the point where the flower was and not *above* it; this is a natural continuation of the old stem which ceased growing at the end of the previous season. It will be noticed when cutting in the spring that a little green tip has already sprouted above the faded flowers; the fact that this has to come off in cutting makes no difference.

I hold the view that systematic trimming in March or early April each year is a key to successful heather cultivation. It can be done even when the weather is frosty. You have only to visit a garden which has been cared for in this way to see how much better it is than one neglected.

LABOUR SAVING

It has already been stated that heathers are invaluable labour-savers. True enough, but the statement requires qualification. While there are spaces between the plants weeds are bound to appear, although for the time being and until the plants grow larger the spaces could be partly filled with various fairly low-growing annuals. As the plants develop they will cover more ground, when the seeds from common weeds will have very little room to germinate. In a well-established heather garden the survival of a few seedling weeds is doubtful, as the heathers just close in and choke them.

Autumn leaves are beneficial when dug into the soil.

PLANTING TIME

April and May are the best spring months for receiving plants from a nursery; no more planting should be done after the third week in May, and even then it is on the late side. Plants may also be ordered in October and November. Two conditions should be noted. First, quick evaporation of moisture after planting *late* in the spring and early *sharp* frosts in the autumn. If the ground is frosty or in a waterlogged condition when the plants arrive, leave them in the box until the weather is more favourable.

The rapid drying out of some plants which come from a nursery in May can be a source of trouble, and occasional losses are known to occur. It is no use writing to the nursery and blaming them. The problem lies at your end. I have mentioned before that should the soil be on the dry side and the atmosphere exceptionally warm for the time of the year it is advisable to work thoroughly wet peat round the roots at the time of planting. Leaf-mould is by no means as good as peat, as I find it dries out in the summer and contains far too many weed seeds, particularly buttercup, germinating freely and producing a crop of seedlings which become a nuisance. In the granulated peat left in the open here for years there are no weeds at all; even grass seeds fail to germinate in it.

To return to moisture evaporation of "new arrivals" in late spring, while the peat is bound to be beneficial to the roots, I do not advocate continual overhead watering of plants during a warm spell, as evaporation is all the more rapid with this method. Once the nursery plants have received a good watering immediately after planting they should be covered lightly with foliage, such as branches of evergreens, lawn mowings, grasses and the like. This will help to conserve moisture and keep much of the hot sun off the plants. It is well to refrain from further watering on the plant itself but to confine this to the soil so as to get down to the roots. Only on extremely rare occasions have I had to resort to such methods; usually the ground has been moist enough for spring planting after the autumn rains and winter snow.

The planter has little to fear in this matter, provided he does not leave the work over until it is almost too late—I find that April is the best of months for all kinds of planting—divisions, transplanting and dealing with fresh lots from a nursery.

When ordering heathers request delivery by passenger train, giving the name of your railway station or nearest station. This ensures delivery on the day following dispatch or no later than the day after, where the destination is at some considerable distance. Some firms send plants by goods train unless the customer stipulates otherwise, and I have known them be on the way for seven days, which is too long a period for heathers. A small consignment, up to 15 lbs. in weight, may come through the post.

I have always found roots pretty well saturated, with damp moss round them, and the plants in first-class condition when they have come from a nursery of repute. I have yet to lodge a complaint. Some firms cover the roots with peat, though it does not follow they are grown in this mixture. They take great care in lifting the plants from their beds and much pride in packing, which has become almost a fine art at one Derbyshire nursery with which I have long done business. It is saying something for their skill when it takes nearly as long to unpack a crate as it does to plant!

When the plants are taken out of the bale be sure not to disturb the soil round the roots; handle them with care if they should arrive with the roots all loose and little soil; then it is a case of bad transplanting in the nursery, and the roots will require a thorough soaking. Have everything ready for immediate transplanting: the right tool for the job, the ground prepared, and peat, if it is necessary to use it. Heathers which have been in transit should not be left about the place, as they will soon dry out, with fatal results. Not a moment should be lost in planting. If unforeseen circumstances prevent you temporarily from carrying out the work, heel in the plants until you are able to deal with them.

CHAPTER VII

SCHEMES FOR THE HEATHER GARDEN

*'It is not three years since the ground was cleared, and already
the Heath garden has a look of young maturity.'*

Gertrude Jekyll

HEATHERS are best planted in an informal way, and, if there
is room enough, in drifts, having regard to the size of the
plants and their colour blending. There is no need to plant
the whole of the garden with heaths but to choose that part most
suitable for their growth—preferably an open sunny situation.

THE ROCKERY

It may consist almost entirely of heathers, with appropriate shrubs
(to which reference will be made later) or the plants might well form
part of and so contribute towards what has already been prepared,
a rockery, for example. It is true that one comes across the *carnea*
heaths in some rockeries, but the others, *cinerea, ciliaris* and *vagans*
are for some inexplicable reason rarely to be found there. Few
people seem to realise that among a group of rocks, jagged and
irregular, heaths and dwarf shrubs have a telling effect. If the
ground rises so much the better, as heathers look well on sloping
land where there is a complete absence of uniformity. One pictures
a group of *cinerea atropurpurea* with the golden *Hypericum poly-
phyllum*.

It is a mistake to imagine that rockeries are intended solely for
alpines and rock plants, for I can think of no others better suited
to this kind of garden than the heaths and heathers. Their foliage
and flower colours blend with stone and they love to throw up a
picturesque seedling from a cranny. I live in a county of millstone
grit, where some of the best flowering heathers of the wild are to
be found growing precariously in the chinks of quarries. The
heather garden rockery is not a fancy idea but a scheme which can
be given practical shape.

Sometimes one or two odd heathers are seen dotted here and
there in a rockery; this is only tinkering. A better plan is bold

66

grouping, especially where the background stands out as a prominent eminence. In our rockery patches of *carnea* spread like carpets over yards of stone, and there are strong tufts of *vagans*, sturdy shapes of *Hammondii*, *Alportii*, C. W. Nix, *flore pleno*—all these are to the rear on rising ground near to long drifts of common heather sprawling over rocks, with a background of *Escallonia langleyensis*, *Senecio Greyi*, berberis and other shrubs. The object aimed at is rugged boldness.

Generally speaking, in the average rockery—and this applies to the lower portion of ours—dwarf forms should be grown, such as *Erica carnea*, *Tetralix*, *cinerea*, *ciliaris*, *vagans Kevernensis alba*, and *Calluna vulgaris minor*, *pumila*, *minima*, and *Foxii*. The taller varieties already mentioned should be planted at the back. One feature should not be lost sight of, that of colour to brighten the winter scene, and in addition to the early flowering carneas I would not hesitate to include the two hybrids, *darleyensis* and George Rendall whose warm, rosy bells seen in the hoar frost and pale sunlight of a February morning are as cheerful to behold as a warm hearth in a cosy lounge. I would include also the *mediterranea* heaths W. T. Rackliff, of pure white bloom, and Brightness, the dark green foliage and rose-coloured flowers relieving the more sombre tone of the stones.

As to the plants to cover the whole rockery, a good deal depends on its size and situation, so that selection is left to individual choice. Some suggestions are made, however, at the end of this chapter. A little crumbling loam mixed with pebbles and peat when planting is all one needs to bother about, for here the plants are not growing in open beds of the garden where the soil is deeper and richer but among rocks with soil much poorer and far less in quantity. Like their companions on the quarry face, the plants, *cinerea*, *ciliaris* and others will grow more slowly compared with others, and if they do not appear quite as robust as those elsewhere in the garden the flowers will be of the best and plentiful.

BEDDING

As a change from roses and annuals, usually seen in a diamond-shaped plot cut out of the lawn, a bed consisting of heathers would not be out of place. One bed is sufficient; it would look more effective than a number, as the other beds consist of plants of an

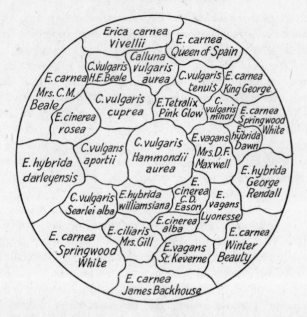

Geometrical beds suitable for making in grass or surrounded with stone paving. The circular bed contains mainly low-growing varieties; the oval one is relatively larger, and grouped round a tall *Erica arborea*.

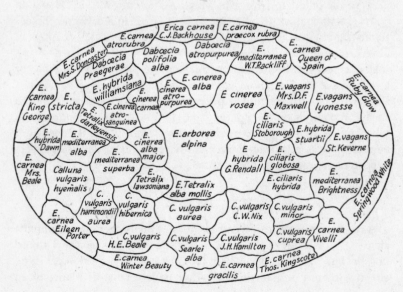

entirely different nature. After all, the real charm of a garden is in
contrasts, pleasing to the eye at every turn, and sometimes appearing
quite elusive in certain lights. The heather bed would provide
colour when roses were out of bloom and annuals had faded away.
Should the owner of the garden have a sentimental feeling in some
mysterious way associated with Scots mythology, then why not
a bed of white heathers? It need only be a small one, with a background of trees and shrubs such as the copper beech, the purple
barberry (*Berberis Thunbergii atropurpurea*), *Prunus cerasifera
Pissardii*—something of a darker shade which would afford relief
to the mass of white which might have, in the absence of such a
background, a glaring effect in the strong sunlight of an
August day.

In the centre of the bed plant *Hammondii aurea*, the tallest of the
whites, or a single specimen of *arborea alpina* (for spring bloom),
provided the bed is a fairly large one, as the tree heath must have
room for liberal expansion. The *Hammondii* follows *arborea*, flowering in July and August; next, Mair's Variety to flower after the
Hammondiis, succeeded by *Searlei alba*. The remaining part of the
bed could be filled with *alba plena* and *torulosa*, and round the
edges *minor* and *pumila*. Add to these *carnea* Springwood White and
Mrs Cecilia M. Beale, *mediterranea* W. T. Rackliff and *Tetralix
alba* to produce blooms in the winter, spring and early summer
before the heathers referred to begin to flower. The number of
plants will depend on the amount of ground available, the larger ones
spaced eighteen inches apart and the small size a foot to a foot and
a half. Plenty of room should be allowed for the sprawling habit of
the carneas.

A bed consisting wholly of white heathers is not everybody's
choice, but its possibilities should not be ruled out. It is important
to bear in mind the position of the bed in relation to other subjects
of the garden and to choose a harmonious background.

Instead of whites, a bed of one variety of a telling rich colour
such as *vagans* Mrs D. F. Maxwell or *Calluna Alportii* would present a gay picture on the lawn. I remember seeing at Kew, across the
green where the heath sand heathers are grown, spacious beds
of that magnificent heather, H. E. Beale. It was June when I
came across the plants—how well they must look in August and
September.

There are so many varieties that one is spoilt for choice in

selecting mixed colours in an open bed; infinite possibilities which
present themselves must be left to individual taste, and a few
suggestions for the reader's guidance are made at the end of this
chapter.

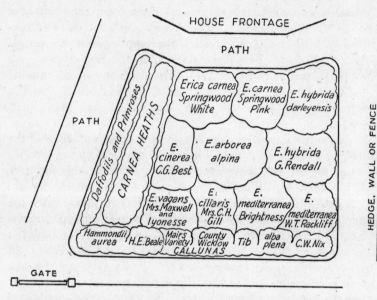

A suggestion for a suburban front garden devoted to heaths.

THE SHRUBBERY

Another suitable site is the fringe of a shrubbery, even in the
shrubbery itself provided the trees are well spaced and not too big.
Heathers have a perfectly natural setting among rhododendrons,
kalmias, pernettyas, berberis, maples, *Rhus Cotinus*, Japanese
flowering cherries, *Senecio Greyi, Ulex europaeus flore pleno* (double
gorse), genistas and many others, not forgetting the tree heaths. A
shrubbery of so many subjects must be of liberal dimensions, to
provide ample space for each tree and plant—there should be no
overcrowding.

In a woodland garden with thick undergrowth of matured trees,
heathers look well on the fringe beside the path where the sun's rays
fall upon them and the light is reasonably good. The gardener who

possesses a shrubbery will find how accommodating the heathers are when it comes to planting (plants for a coppice adjoining the garden are referred to later in this chapter).

EDGINGS, CARPETING AND PATHS

Low-growing heaths, the carneas, for example, are excellent plants for edging. There is no need to get the line out and make it dead straight. Edges look better when the plants are like mats sprawling somewhat irregularly beside a path or lawn or border. Each plant should be placed a foot apart and allowed to run its own course without resorting to pruning. Trim straggling portions occasionally. A good example is to be found in the approach to King William's Temple at Kew gardens, where hundreds of carneas are edging plants to the path. The two golden Callunas, *aurea* and *Searlei aurea*, are suitable for this purpose and present a delightful picture in the spring. Carpeting heaths over the scrub of a woodland and little patches of ground in odd nooks and corners of the garden solve a problem of knowing just what to plant in such places. They are blessed with three cardinal virtues. First, as cheerful evergreens, second, as colourful objects when in flower, and third, as labour-savers in helping to keep down weeds.

Even a path which is not the main way from the road to the house, but a link between one part of the garden and another, may be clothed with heathers. It should be well weeded before any planting is done, and after the surface is dressed with peat (two-thirds) and sand (one-third) common heathers (*Calluna vulgaris*) are planted eighteen inches apart. As the plants will get as tough as a brush tail they will stand walking over with little injury, and once a year, late in the autumn, when the blooms have faded, the path is mown. If the plants are not much beyond the seedling stage, mowing need not begin until two years later.

A BED OF HEATHERS

By the road on the south side of our garden is a triangular shrubbery flanked by a path from the lower gate to the terrace surrounding the house. A mixed border lies on the other side of the path, leading to the rose beds and lawns, with shrubs in the background and groups of astilbes, spireas and hypericums in the

centre. Further north the lawn is broken by cultivated ground, a
bed, 27 feet long and 10 feet wide, consisting solely of heaths and
heathers which can be seen in an elevated position from the front
of the house, the entire ground sloping and forming part of a hillside nearly 1000 feet above sea level.

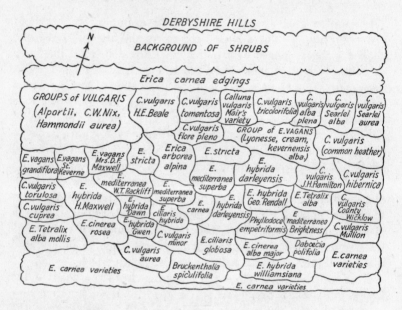

Plan of one of the author's heather gardens

In the centre of the heather garden is the tree heath, *arborea
alpina*, which is given ample space for growth; on each side of it is
stricta, the Corsican heath, one being planted a little further to the
north than the other (there are no straight lines in the heather
garden), and *mediterranea superba*. There are also the two hybrids,
Darleyensis and George Rendall. To the left, or west side, from the
centre, is a group of *vagans*, varieties Mrs D. F. Maxwell, St
Keverne, and *grandiflora*; and between them and the carneas which
are edging plants by the lawn we find *Calluna vulgaris torulosa*,
cuprea and *minor*, *Tetralix alba mollis*, *cinerea rosea*, and *Brucken-
thalia spiculifolia*. To the right from the centre, on the east side,
is another group of *vagans*, Lyonesse, Cream, and *Kevernensis
alba*, and from them to the carneas at the front we see

the callunas J. H. Hamilton, County Wicklow, and Mullion, *mediterranea* Brightness, *cinerea alba major, ciliaris globosa,* the hybrid *Williamsiana, Daboëcia polifolia alba,* and *Phyllodoce empetriformis.*

In the background, on the north side, are groupings of callunas, *Alportii,* C. W. Nix, *Hammondii,* Mair's Variety, *aurea, flore pleno, Searlei alba* and *S. aurea, alba plena, hibernica* and one or two others.

All are planted irregularly about eighteen inches apart, excepting the *arborea, mediterranea* and *stricta*—and there is bloom all the year round. The grouping of one variety is the best way of planting as each displays a fine show of flowers when seen in a mass. One should observe also the effective contrast in foliage, three or four of the hybrid Dawn presenting a charming picture beside the hybrid George Rendall—the pink blossoms, golden-tipped stems, and mossy green leaves of Dawn against the stronger and deeper shade of the Rendall which is freely covered with ivory-tinted buds, although the plant will not flower until well in the New Year. Then there is the coppery hue of *Calluna vulgans cuprea* late in the year against the more sombre *cinerea rosea,* the golden heads of *Williamsiana* against *Darleyensis,* the very deep *carnea Vivellii* by the lively green *stricta,* the lilac sprays of *hibernica* above the *carnea* King George, and so on.

The above scheme (by no means perfect in colour grouping) provides a basis for working ideas which can be developed. It is the kind of heather garden one has in mind for the average gardener.

HEDGES

How often do we see a hedge of heathers? Very rarely. Conventions remain without any thought of trying something new—conventions that belong to a period in which the dull features of box, laurel and privet screened us from our neighbour's domain. Few of us realise how charming a hedge of *vagans* heaths can be, giving little trouble in the way of maintenance beyond an annual pruning with the shears. One is not suggesting heaths for external boundary hedges where the length is considerable—they call for beech or berberis or thorn—but for those of a moderate size which divide one section of the garden from another, hedges that help to break up uniformity and make some contribution to picturesque harmony.

The variety of heath or heather to be chosen should be carefully considered according to the position of the hedge, i.e. you would avoid planting *stricta* in a spot exposed to cold winds from the east, and a hedge of the calluna *Alportii* is hardly suitable if adjacent to a mixed border, as the crimson colour when the hedge is in full flower would be too marked against the colours in the border. The tree heath, *arborea*, makes a splendid hedge, but it should only be grown as such in a mild and favourable part of the country. *Arborea alpina* is more dependable and less liable to injury in a severe winter. The only snag about these two plants for a hedge of fair length is the cost, as tree heaths are much dearer to buy from nurseries than the average heather plant. One has to study the economic side.

Stricta is cheaper and quite satisfactory for this purpose; each plant should be spaced some two feet apart to provide a hedge three to four feet in height, and the whole upon maturity would have quite an artistic effect, the moss-green leaves being so bright and conspicuous in the sunlight, and the clusters of pale rose at the tip of the tree adding a finishing touch to this beautiful heath. A hedge of *stricta* should not be pruned until the spring, then only judiciously, to avoid a straggling appearance, for the plant has a mellowed dignity in the faded russet blooms during the winter months.

Another heath admirably suited for a hedge is *vagans*, because of its pleasing foliage throughout the whole year. Probably the most symmetrical of all heaths under cultivation, this feature stands out perfectly in a hedge. One I recall was planted many years ago; it is 45 yards long, 2 feet wide, and 15 inches high, each plant being spaced a foot apart. The hedge is close-clipped, neat and maintained in excellent condition. There are no blooms owing to cutting. Another *vagans* hedge (illustration, page 42) has been left to grow, and, although full of flower, has not the tidy appearance of the other. One should choose, according to individual ideas or taste, whether the hedge must be kept regularly trimmed and so lose the bloom, or cut back once a year after the flowering period is over. For my own part, I like to see the faded corolla of reddish brown of both *stricta* and *vagans* contributing to the winter garden, and prune in early spring before new growth begins.

THE BORDER

The past twenty years have seen so many introductions of herbaceous plants that the border is in danger of being overstocked, and as many of these subjects make strong root and occupy a good deal of space there seems little left for heathers. Some of the choice varieties of *cinerea* and *ciliaris* are so dwarfed by tall border plants that their identity almost becomes lost and they are best excluded. Only heaths of vigorous growth, such as *vagans grandiflora*, and the calluna H. E. Beale are able to hold their own amid such rival company (the last-named holds its own anywhere).

Winter and early spring heaths are better for the border for they will flower when few other plants are in bloom and they look well among daffodils, Christmas roses, and snowdrops. The carneas Springwood White, King George, *Vivellii*, Winter Beauty, *gracilis* and James Backhouse, *mediterranea* W. T. Rackliff, Brightness, the hybrids *Darleyensis* and George Rendall—these will furnish the border with bloom at intervals from January to May and so keep it well filled with flowers. Another feature to remember is the attractive foliage of the heaths during the summer and autumn months.

Is there provision made for heathers in the average border? I doubt it. But there ought to be if only as a contribution to the winter garden.

GRASS PLOTS

I have pleasant memories of a beautiful heather garden at Union Mills in the Isle of Man. On the left-hand side of a winding, rising path at the back of the house, a stretch of rough grassland slopes gradually for some 30 yards and is roughly 10 yards wide, although the width varies in places. The background consists of many fine trees and shrubs (which should be a feature of every heather garden because they enhance the natural beauty of the scene)— *Cupressus macrocarpa*, double pink cherries (*Prunus Cerasus*), white poplar (*Populus alba*), *Prunus Pissardii*, and others.

The remainder of the ground is devoted entirely to heaths and heathers, space being allowed for walking round the plants, the turf dug out where each heather is planted and the grass cut twice a year. The grouping is magnificent, consisting of fine specimens of *vagans*, *carnea* and *cinerea* varieties, *ciliaris*, *Callunas*, *mediterranea* and *Daboëcia*; at the back are *arborea* and *australis*.

It was my good fortune to see this garden in September when thousands of blooms smothered the plants. The owner had developed it over a period of some years and was very proud of what the heathers had done for her. Among its most attractive features which appealed to me immensely were the picturesque blending colours of the Irish *Daboëcia polifolia alba* and *atropurpurea* mixed with the charming purple and white *bicolor*; the hundreds of blooms of a soft lilac shade in a single plant of *Calluna hibernica* (in flower a month earlier than it is with me); and the new *Daboëcia Praegerae* from Connemara swaying its large and very beautiful flushed pink bells in the breeze, and where the bloom had still to appear the buds were of deep pink; and the enormous long sprays of the *Calluna elegantissima* full of buds which seemed almost ready to break into blossom. Owing to the abnormal by drysummer the plants were flowering in advance of the normal season.

This Manx garden provides a simple illustration of what can be done with a stretch of turf upon which scores of heathers grow perfectly. There is no reason why it should not be done on similar lines in other gardens; its labour-saving value alone should appeal to many, for, except for the cutting of the grass once in six months and occasional trimming of the plants, there is nothing further to be done. It is a model of informal gardening at its best.

One thing I noticed was the countless number of seedlings, particularly of *vagans*, in the grass and along the path—enough plants to begin a new garden!

From these various schemes it will be made clear that heathers are adaptable to most parts of the garden. The carneas above all are most accommodating and will grow under trees, provided they are deciduous with the lowest branches not less than fifteen feet from the ground. *Vagans* also will prosper in part shade. Carneas may be planted between the bushes in a rose bed to bring colour into that part of the garden which is bare in the winter. This should be done without overcrowding the bed and where plenty of space is to be found between the trees, as the plot has to be walked over at pruning time. The carneas would certainly keep down the weeds. There should be no planting where fresh manure has been freely applied over the surface, as the ammonia is too strong for the roots of heaths. It is safe enough after a time where the manure has been well dug in.

COLOUR GROUPING

The general arrangement of the plants and the selection of suitable colours must be left largely to individual taste, for what appeals to one does not always impress another. I am frankly of the opinion that the keen woman planter has a more catholic outlook on a garden scheme than a man, whose loyalty to orthodox ideas is not easily broken. I have seen women who (dare one say, literally!) "know their onions" about the garden and who have not hesitated to embark on planting which, to some men, seemed like sacrilege in a world traditionally formal. Furthermore, the keen plantswoman has a fine perception of colour in the garden, just as she has the gift of choicely arranging cut blooms for decoration in the home.

In colour grouping the size of the site has to be considered; obviously half an acre of land would be planned differently from a small garden. Quite apart from colours, it is advisable to allow a liberal margin between the plants, never less than the scale as detailed at the end of this chapter. The main object is to aim at bold groupings of one variety, the colours of which will be seen to full advantage during the flowering period. Drifts of the callunas *Alportii* and C. W. Nix, David Eason and Tib, respond to this treatment, and how well they look against a background of *Hypericum Henryi* and *H. grandiflorum*.

One does not call for a blaze of colour, like a bed of annuals in midsummer, but simple harmonies of tone which do not offend the eye. A break here and there of a white to relieve the strong shade of rich crimson is an example of the kind of selection one has in mind. These crimsons, to be found in the cinereas and ciliaris, are hardly in harmony with the strong purples of the callunas and they should not be grown together—the clash is too marked.

The warm bright rose of *cinerea rosea* is pleasing with the pretty sprays of *c. torulosa*; the bright carmine of *cinerea coccinea* with the white of *c. minor. Lilacina* would not be overwhelmed by the purple blooms of *c. aurea* as the latter are few in number and the cheerful golden leaves of the heather make a pleasant background to the lilac cinerea. Another *cinerea*, Apple Blossom, has shell-pink bells but the paler pink hybrid, Gwen, would not neutralise the colours to render ineffective the more delicate shade of the Apple Blossom—a stronger pink, such as the hybrid, H. Maxwell, might easily do so. The pure white of the vigorous grower, *vagans* Lyonesse could be grouped together, choosing C. W. Nix as a strong crimson background.

The foliage of a plant in a season when it is not in bloom affords a natural break to one that is in flower, or about to flower. Take the following: the bronze leaves of *carnea Vivellii* and the deep green of *mediterranea* Brightness against *stricta*'s bright colour and pink bells on the tip of the tall upright stems. Around the base of the tree heath, *Veitchii*, a patch of C. J. H. Hamilton would provide cover; the dark foliage of the latter in midwinter and early spring is an excellent foil to the lighter shade of the former, and the large, pink flowers of the Hamilton in August have a background of the fresh-looking *Veitchii*. Although these two plants bloom at different seasons, *Veitchii* in the spring, and C. J. H. Hamilton late in the summer, the grouping is admirably suitable throughout the year.

Variations of this kind come readily to the planter who derives pleasure from the heathers which go well together and blend naturally to their surroundings. There is no need to be too sticklish about colour schemes with so wide a range to choose from.

Before making a heather garden on a larger scale than has already been described, the landscape as a whole must be reviewed. The garden may be in an open situation, or part of a woodland dell, planted with conifers or quite formal with lawns and terraces. In a coppice adjacent to the main garden we find rhododendrons, larches, firs, saplings of birch and beech, brooms, gorse and bracken. Here is a natural setting for *mediterranea superba* and tree heaths, bringing fragrance and flower in early spring.

A few feet of the rough undergrowth must be cleared before a heath is planted and the bramble and gorse, weeds removed—a job for pick and axe in addition to fork and spade. Heathers planted come near to nature's handiwork of the woodland where foxglove, harebell and wild grasses grow by winding paths through bracken and gorse.

I will return to this subject later in describing those shrubs closely allied to the heath family and introduce ideas for developing the heather garden on more comprehensive lines.

So far I have endeavoured to stimulate interest on behalf of the

An informal planting of *Erica carnea*, the hardiest of heaths, which flowers during winter.

Erica carnea Vivellii has carmine flowers and foliage which turns reddish in the winter.

The Springwood varieties of *E. carnea*, of which this is the white, are among the most vigorous.

Above: A drift of the bell heather, *E. cinerea;* this is the red-flowered variety C. D. Eason.

Right: The dense, robust growth of *E. cinerea rosea*, one of the oldest varieties.

Above: Erica ciliaris is noteworthy for its pale green foliage. This variety, *rotundifolia*, has pink flowers.

Left: The symmetrical growth of *Erica mediterranea*, Brightness. It has brilliant red flowers.

smaller type of garden, for it is the owners of these in the country or suburb whom I would like to see cultivating these lovely plants.

SUGGESTIONS FOR THE ROCKERY

Erica carnea
Mrs Cecilia M. Beale – *gracilis* – King George – Ruby Glow – Springwood White – Springwood Pink – *Vivellii* – Winter Beauty.

Erica ciliaris
hybrida – Mrs C. H. Gill – *globosa* – *rotundifolia.*

Erica cinerea
alba – *alba major* – *atrosanguinea* (Smith's variety) – C. D. Eason – C. G. Best – Frances – Golden Drop – John Eason – *lilacina* – *pallida* – *pygmaea* – Victoria.

Erica mediterranea
Brightness – W. T. Rackliff.

Erica Tetralix
alba mollis – *Darleyensis* – *Lawsoniana* – *Praegeri.*

Erica vagans
Kevernensis alba.

Hybrid Heaths
Darleyensis – George Rendall – Dawn – H. Maxwell – *Williamsiana.*

Calluna vulgaris
aurea – County Wicklow – *coccinea* – *cuprea* – David Eason – *Foxii floribunda* – *minima* – Mullion – *nana compacta* – Mrs Pat – Sister Anne – *tenuis* – Tom Thumb.

BACKGROUND FOR LARGE ROCKERY

Erica vagans
grandiflora – Lyonesse – Mrs D. F. Maxwell – St. Keverne.

Calluna vulgaris
Alportii – *alba plena* – C. W. Nix – *flore pleno* – H. E. Beale – *Hammondii aurea* – Mair's variety – *Searlei alba* – *Searlei aurea.*

SUGGESTIONS FOR BEDDING

Erica carnea – as described in this chapter.

THG   E

Erica ciliaris
hybrida – Mrs C. H. Gill – *Maweana* – Stoborough.

Erica cinerea
atropurpurea – *coccinea* – C. G. Best – P. S. Patrick – Rose Queen.

Erica mediterranea
Brightness – *rosea*.

Erica Tetralix
Praegeri.

Erica vagans
grandiflora – Mrs D. F. Maxwell – St. Keverne.

Hybrid Heaths
Darleyensis – Dawn – H. Maxwell – *Williamsiana*.

Calluna vulgaris
alba plena – *Alportii* – Carlton – County Wicklow – David Eason – E. Hoare – *elegantissima* – H. E. Beale – *hibernica* – J. H. Hamilton – Tib. (And the whites described in this chapter.)

DISTANCES BETWEEN PLANTS

Calluna vulgaris	1½ feet
Erica arborea	4 to 6 feet
E. aborea var, *alpina*	4 to 6 feet
E. australis	4 to 6 feet
E. carnea	1¼ feet
E. ciliaris	1 to 1½ feet
E. cinerea	1 to 1½ feet
E. lusitanica (syn. *codonodes*)	4 to 6 feet
E. mediterranea—	
var. *hibernica*	2 feet
var. *superba*	3 feet
Other varieties	2 feet
E. scoparia	4 to 6 feet
E. stricta	2½ feet
E. Tetralix	¾ to 1½ feet
E. vagans	2 feet

The hybrids *Darleyensis* and George Rendall should each be planted 2 feet apart and the remaining hybrids 1 to 1½ feet. Always allow plenty of room in planting; it pays in the long run. Nothing is more annoying than to be compelled to dig up well-established plants owing to overcrowding; this can be avoided at the outset.

CHAPTER VIII

VARIETIES

Not many plants represented in gardens as large genera have escaped the ministrations of the hybridist, few have resisted the temptation to respond to the cultivator's zeal by diverting from their ancient tribal laws. But the heaths we grow today are as fresh with the breezy delights of their own mist-swept moorlands as if they had never known the softening influences of a cultural life. They are the virgin gold of nature's own mint, and so devoutly do they cling to their ancestral conservatism that the diversions of a cocktail age have no attractions for them. In the garden their racial traditions have never shown a lapse.

A. T. Johnson

IN this chapter the species and varieties of *Calluna, Daboëcia (Menziesia)* and *Erica* are described in alphabetical order.

CALLUNA VULGARIS

(*Greek* Kalluno *to cleanse or adorn, either for the use of its twigs in brooms or for the beauty of its flowers.*)

Common heather or ling is an evergreen upright shrub, varying in height from half a foot, sometimes less, to two feet, rarely more. (Tall heather in parts of Scotland exceeds two feet.)

The leaves are small, downy, deep green and closely imbricated—meaning closely overlapping, one upon another like roof tiles. They are scale-like and oblong-strapped, about half an inch in size. They lie in four longitudinal rows on opposite sides of the stems and branches, each having two small spurs at the base. This overlapping of the leaves enables the plant to conserve moisture which is a natural reserve in a period of drought and of great value when the plant exerts its maximum strength during the long period of bloom in summer and autumn.

Close proximity of leaf distinguishes *Calluna* from *Erica*, the needle-like leaves of the latter being spaced in whorls along the stem. There is no overlapping among the heaths.

The flowers, in long terminal spikes, are arranged in axillary racemes, the calyx of four united sepals being pink or rose-purple (occasionally white), with four green bracts at the base. *Calluna* differs from the heath in having a 4-parted *coloured* calyx, *longer* than the corolla.

Most people who are not gardeners think of heather as they see it in flower as part of a country landscape, without knowing of the varieties which have long been cultivated in the garden. Not a few amateur gardeners have themselves expressed surprise at the extensive range these plants cover, in height, foliage, and flower. There are over 70 in all; 25 white forms, including the Lucky Scotch White, *alba*, 11 purple, 36 red, crimson, lilac or pink and other colours. I mention these figures not for any statistical value which may attach to them but to give the reader an idea of the comprehensive collection under cultivation.

The variations in width and height are considerable. Mrs Ronald Gray, for example, is so prostrate that it can be walked on, and no heather is quite as flat-to-the-ground. Even *minima* is two inches above soil level. At the other extreme *Hammondii* approaches three feet, and, like *Alportii*, *flore pleno* and *Searlei*, grows into a shapely bush. In between are many plants from nine to eighteen inches which are easily cultivated and well suited to the average garden. An important point to remember—the absence of uniformity in heather plants is of value to the man or woman planning an informal scheme. One should mention, also, that the double-flowering varieties, such as *alba plena*, *flore pleno*, H. E. Beale, County Wicklow, J. H. Hamilton and Tib, though limited in number, are plants of first-class reputation, and should be grown even where the owner has no thought of making a heather garden. Such plants as the six mentioned will hold their own in floral beauty no matter in what company they are found.

As no heathers come into flower during the first six months of the year, the heather garden is obviously incomplete if they alone are chosen, without the spring-flowering heaths and the winter carneas. But their contribution in the latter half of the year is so wide that they may be planted in different parts of the garden, quite outside the heather plot.

First to flower, in July, is *tenuis*, the dwarf scarlet heath, soon to be followed by the early white, another dwarf, called *minor*; from then onwards for five months till the end of the year there is a succession of bloom, the varieties *hyemalis* and *elegantissima* completing the seasons of summer and autumn.

There are two dozen white forms of *Calluna vulgaris*, as listed below; before these lines are in print new ones will no doubt be introduced.

alba	July-August	18 *inches*
August Beauty	August-September	1 *foot*
Carlton	August-September	18 *inches*
dumosa	July-September	18 *inches*
elata	September-October	2 *feet*
elegantissima	August-September	2 *feet*
erecta	July-August	18 *inches*
Hammondii	August-September	2 *ft. 6 in.*
Hammondii aurea	August-September	2 *ft. 6 in.*
Hayesensis	August-September	18 *inches*
Kit Hill	September-October	9 *inches*
Mair's variety	August-September	3 *feet*
minor	July-August	6 *inches*
pilosa	August-September	9 *inches*
plena	August-September	18 *inches*
pumila	July-August	9 *inches*
pyramidalis	August-September	2 *feet*
rigida	August-September	1 *foot*
Searlei	September-October	2 *feet*
Searlei aurea	September-October	18 *inches*
spicata	August-September	1 *foot*
tenella	August-September	1 *foot*
tomentosa	September-October	18 *inches*
torulosa	August-September	1 *foot*

As some of the best varieties are described on pages 89-96 no further comment is called for except to emphasise that Carlton, *Hammondii*, Mair's variety, *plena*, *Searlei*, *tomentosa* and *torulosa* are plants of established reputation and well worth growing.

Of the remainder, one would mention that the true Scotch White Heather, the traditional emblem of good luck and good fellowship, is *alba*, which now falls short as a plant of garden merit compared with better and improved forms.

Elata is an improved Scotch White, a bushy plant, late in flowering; it has never produced in Derbyshire the tall and elegant spikes which make it so magnificent a plant in the Lakes.

Some of the others have long been cultivated: *spicata*, a handsome, free-flowering plant; *rigida*, a dwarfer type of stiff, erect growth; *pumila*, a charming, medium-sized white, flowering early with plenty of bloom and foliage, the stems being softer and less twiggy than the common *Calluna vulgaris*; *minor*, of bright green leaves and lots of pretty small sprays; *pilosa*, which has 'misty' looking foliage— actually, it is hairy; also *dumosa* and *tenella*.

Among new varieties is August Beauty of unusual habit. The tops of the stems and flowers curl over and gradually droop downwards as though making their way back to the base of the plant to complete the circle. Also new is Kit Hill, blooming freely in the autumn, with flowers on the laterals as well as on the curving spikes. *Hayesensis* is another less familiar variety, with long spikes of pure white bloom. A continental grower is sending me a white *elegantissima*, of which, at the time of writing, I have no knowledge.

VARIETIES OF CALLUNA VULGARIS

Alportii   August-September   2 *feet*

A small bush of upright habit, sage-green leaves, rich crimson flowers fading to warm russet in autumn and early winter.

Alportii praecox   July-August   18 *inches*

If you would like earlier blooms this variety will provide them; flowers about three weeks before the older form. In growing both, the Alportiis have a flowering period of well over three months.

argentea /   August-September   9-12 *inches*

The silver foliage in my plants is not as marked as I had been led to suppose from some published descriptions. Tips of the leaves are of a very pale green, almost white when examined closely, and viewed from normal eye level this contrast of green shades in a bed of plants creates an illusory silvery cast. It is not a variety to

write home about and the blooms are few and disappointing.
Purple flowers.

aurea   August-September   1 *foot*

A beautiful foliage plant with slender feathery stems, bright gold
in the spring, toned down during the summer months and turning
to deep red in the winter. Purple blooms, limited in number.

Camla variety   August-September   9 *inches*

Similar to County Wicklow, perhaps a better form, as the double
pink blossoms are larger and the spikes invariably longer.

coccinea   August-September   9 *inches*

Scarlet to deep crimson flowers, grey foliage. An excellent plant
provided you obtain the true form and not the one less deep in
colour sometimes displayed at shows. Smith's variety, so long
established, is the best I have seen.

County Wicklow   August-September   9 *inches*

Prostrate, of twiggy habit, laden with double, shell-pink flowers,
and one of the best heathers. It has long been a favourite. Should
be propagated from cuttings, as the hard woody stems are
unsuitable for layering.

Cronix   August-September   18 *inches*

This deep red flowering variety is new to me and some plants have
only recently arrived. It is a tall, handsome heather, of graceful
foliage, with rich, deep bronze and green leaves. I wonder if the
name is a misprint for C.W. Nix.

cuprea   August-September   6 *inches*

From the window of the room in which I am writing these notes
in early March I can see a bed of cuprea plants. These appear more
prominent than most of the other heathers as the leaves are
a bright red—an unusual colour for the time of the year—and all
the more effective when the sun is shining on them. Like *aurea*, it
depends on foliage for distinction, especially as the coppery shade
deepens in the winter time. The few purple blooms count for little;
the value of the plant is its contribution to the winter garden.

crasmeriensis   August-September   1 *foot*

Pink flowers along the whole of the stem, with long erect spikes.
Free blooming. Not very well known and should be more widely
grown.

C. W. Nix August-September *2 feet*
More graceful in its feathery stems than *Alportii* and brighter in bloom. The flowers are a hot crimson.

Darleyensis August-September *18 inches*
When this plant was introduced from Scotland to a Derbyshire nursery it was wrongly labelled as *tenuis*, and as it had no title the name of *Darleyensis* was given to it. Small pinky-red bells cluster on curly-headed tips, the tussocks being unusual among heathers.

David Eason October-November *1 foot*
Light green foliage; a reddish coloured flower with a tinge of purple, the red being more pronounced and deeper as the bloom matures.

E. Hoare August-September *18 inches*
Rich, deep crimson, though not a true crimson—there is a touch of purple in it.

elegantissima October-December *2 feet*
Long spikes, up to fourteen inches, of soft lilac flowers, tapering to a fine point, which give the plant its apt and well-deserved name. Without doubt the most beautiful and certainly the most graceful heather I have come across. In full bloom when all others, excepting *hyemalis*, have faded. Not proved hardy everywhere and is injured by keen frosts in an early winter.

flore pleno August-October *18 inches*
First of the double lings to be cultivated. The spikes are not as long as H. E. Beale nor the colour of the flower as lively. When the bud breaks the pretty bell is of a soft pink shade which does not deepen as much as the purple varieties and in full flower the blending tones of pink and lilac contribute to the shrub's charm.

Foxii floribunda August-September *4 inches*
Foxii nana *3 inches*
I grow a few odd plants of these curious Foxiis. They form round mats, shaped so perfectly as to lead one to imagine that they had been clipped in the night by a band of elves amusingly interested in horticulture, or they might even be a fairy bush for the little imps to dance round. *F. floribunda* occasionally unfolds a pinky-mauve flower; the remaining blooms are stolen, I think, by the moonlight visitors. The flowers are purple in *F. nana*.

Goldsworth Crimson   October-November   2 *feet*
A rich crimson autumn flower, in full bloom in November. The
erect, stiff branches and sage-green foliage are like Alportii, but
over a score of years I have found it very shy in bloom with only
a few bells near the tips of the spikes. A good plant to look at;
otherwise rather disappointing.

Hammondii rubrifolia   August-September   18 *inches*
My own seedlings from beds of *Hammondii* (which is a white)
occasionally produce a purple flower and the plants show much
promise. The foliage of the seedlings varies from the green of the
Hammondii to the golden of the *aurea* form; one grower has introduced a plant with bright red in the spring's new growth and
named it *H. rubrifolia*. These seedlings provide interesting breaks
from the familiar white.

H. E. Beale   August-October   2 *feet*
So well known is this plant that any description of it seems
unnecessary, and it is referred to in more detail in the chapter of
Choice Heathers (page 35). We see and welcome it in gardens without any pretence to heather cultivation. Not only are the long-
spiked flowers unrivalled in their beautiful display of silvery-pink
rosettes but they appear in such abundance, on nearly all the
laterals as well as the stems. Every garden lover fortunate enough
to possess this plant will appreciate the Award of Merit given to
it by the R.H.S. Considered the best of the species.

hibernica   October-November   6 *inches*
Bearing in mind that this plant is no more than six inches high, the
number of blooms is enormous. I doubt if there is another of half-
a-foot stature to equal it in this respect. I have just been looking
at a bed in March and find the faded corollas are so numerous that
the foliage is largely hidden. The long, lovely bright lilac sprays
precede the flowers of *hyemalis*, and the two combined provide
the finishing touches of the heather season. Even as late as March
the faded flowers look like white heather in bloom at the wrong
time of the year.

Hookstone   August-September   2 *feet*
This fairly new, tall and sturdy plant bears pink flowers.

hyemalis   October-December   9 *inches*
The last heather to bloom in our garden, its bud opening about the
end of October and sometimes in November. I have never known
abrupt changes in the weather, gale winds or sharp overnight frost
to injure the bloom. It is in perfect flower on the shortest day of
the year and continues well into January. The charming pinky-lilac
blossom appears at a time when the floral year is much subdued
in colour.

hypnoides   August-September   1 *foot*
Purple flowers of medium quality, a plant rarely seen now as
other varieties have overshadowed it.

J. H. Hamilton   August-September   9 *inches*
A double flower of diffused pink, quite different from the shade one
finds in the Co. Wicklow and H. E. Beale class. When it first comes
into flower the pink, in cheerful contrast to the dark, sombre leaves,
is distinctly bright and in September a warm glowing colour. No
purple at all in this heather, which received an Award of Merit from
the R.H.S.

Kynance   August-September   1 *foot*
Kynance Cove with its fine beach and rocks in Cornwall is not far
from Mullion—and here we have two plants with Cornish names, the
former, Kynance, being a few inches taller than the latter, Mullion,
and a lighter pink. Very free blooming.

minima   August-September   2 *inches*
At one time this was recognised as the smallest heather in cultivation, being only a couple of inches above ground; now it is out-
rivalled by the one-inch Mrs Ronald Gray. Seen in the light of
dusk *minima* could be taken for a young hedgehog. Probably the
closest-growing stems among heathers, as they are in mass formation and bind into a solid mat. Unfortunately the purple blooms
are few.

Mrs Pat   August-September   6 *inches*
Light green foliage, seen at its best in the spring. Tiny pink tips
to the shoots, mauve pink bud and light purple flowers; a fine
dwarf, bushy variety.

Mrs Ronald Gray   August-September   1 *inch*
An excellent prostrate plant with a strong twiggy habit, and pretty
reddish flowers. Quite uncommon. Never settled down with me
although I have seen it quite happy not far away. Why it has not
developed in our soil and why it is so miserable in midwinter I
cannot understand. Probably severe frosts considerably damage the
roots which are near the surface.

Mullion   August-September   9 *inches*
Low and close-growing, deep pink flowers; one of the best of the
small-size heathers. Not as hardy as some, as it 'browns off' in a
hard winter but soon recovers in the spring.

nana compacta   August-September   3 *inches*
One or two dwarfs fail to produce blooms in sufficient number to
justify their existence; this one is an exception and almost makes up
for what some of the others fail to give us. Scores of tiny pink flowers
clothe the plant, giving it the name of the 'pin-cushion heather'. I
regard *n. compacta* as the best in the lilliputian group.

pallida   August-September   1 *foot*
Rarely seen these days because newer introductions are considered
more attractive and appeal to growers' customers. For this reason
a plant such as *pallida* is no longer listed. It is a pity, for unless we
are careful some of the older forms will disappear altogether, as
nurserymen have ceased to propagate from them. As I think *pallida*
is one that should be preserved, I have been raising fresh stock for
some time. It is a soft, diffused purple with a slight trace of pink
and not so pale as to be washed out altogether. Well worth a place
in the sun again.

prostrata Kuphaldtii   August-September   1 *inch*
A creeping plant reminding me of Mrs Ronald Gray; rosy purple
flowers.

pygmaea   August-September   3 *inches*
Another dwarf, closely-growing plant; dark green foliage, and a few
purple flowers.

Roma   August-September   9 *inches*
I have not had this new variety long enough to form an opinion
but the flowers are a deep pink and it looks an attractive plant.

salmonoides   August-September   1 *foot*
A sturdy heather, erect foliage and flowers a salmon shade. As it
bloomed so well last summer I thought the plant should be seen more
than it is and, as in the case of *pallida*, I am increasing the stock.

Searlei rubra   September-October   2 *feet*
A valuable heather because it flowers well and late. A break from
the familiar white form, displaying pinky-red flowers and losing
none of the graceful, feathery foliage which makes *Searlei* so handsome a plant.

Silver Queen   August-September   1 *foot*
Woolly, silvery-green leaves, lavender flowers, and rather shy in
bloom. A new variety.

Sister Anne   August-September   2-3 *inches*
This is one of those curious kinds of heather, which, at a glance,
do not look like a heather at all. It is a mere crinkled tuft, calling
for microscopical observation. To describe it as a carpeter is to be
prosaic. The silvery grey leaves, growing more horizontally than
vertically, tone down during the autumn and assume a reddish
cast in the winter. Then, to add to the eccentric behaviour, pretty
pink flowers curl at the tip as though admiring the plant as a whole,
like a girl peeping through a mirror to admire her beauty. A more
unusual heather I have yet to see—quite a floral curiosity, and the
name itself is just as intriguing.

tenuis   July-September   6 *inches*
Known as the Scarlet Heath, the first to bloom, and has a long
flowering season. For a dwarf the flowers of reddish-purple are
many, the fading bells deepen to a rich warm red, and it is one of
the oldest and one of the best of heathers.

Tib   August-September   1 *foot*
A delightful plant with rich green foliage, and long spikes of rosy
crimson. The double flowers are clustered along the stem.

Tom Thumb   August-September   6 *inches*
A mossy little fellow, with fresh golden-green foliage and compact
leaves. Looks like a conifer escaped from a Japanese garden. This
beautiful plant of pink blossoms is uncommon in habit, foliage and
bloom.

tricolorifolia   August-September   1 *foot*
(Smith's variety)

The combination of colour in the spring foliage is unique. Tips of
the stems are a light coppery pink and golden, the remainder of the
plant green. Purple flowers. A seedling discovered on the Flash
nursery of James Smith & Son, Darley Dale. It is a plant often
admired by my friends in April and May.

Underwoodii   August-November   1 *foot*

Long slender spikes of silvery pink buds open in August to lavender-
mauve flowers, which turn to deep purple in October and November. A new and beautiful heather which is sure to be widely grown
when better known.

DABOËCIA CANTABRICA

syn. D. polifolia and Menziesia polifolia—St Dabeoc's Heath
(*Latin* Cantabricus, *a region of Northern Spain formerly inhabited by
the Cantabri.*).

Differing in some of the characteristics associated with the
heath family, this Irish shrub infuses colour and charm as well as
a rambling, informal habit on an elevated sunny bank amid thymes,
pernettyas, foxgloves and ferns. It also brings out its full beauty in
sun and shadow, on the fringe of a woodland, and is seen to the
best effect when the varieties are grown together with the colours
mingling one with another.

Sometimes cut to the ground in a severe winter, as these plants
were at Wisley in 1947 (I saw them later in June making a good
recovery) their general hardiness is uncertain. Experience has
proved that in open ground which provides no protection from
north and east winds in the winter these plants are liable to be
killed. They will not endure a prolonged dry period in early spring
when the soil is caked hard and the surface like dust, when there is
an absence of moisture that is so essential for their well-being. Such
unnatural conditions are fatal to the Irish bog heath of Connemara.

To keep them immune from injury in exposed places there are
two things to be done. First, to grow them in peat; second, to provide adequate shelter. In an exposed north-country nursery high
beech hedges break the winds.

As my stock is considerable and as I cannot afford to suffer losses
which have occurred in open ground in some winters of the past,
I protect most of the plants in frames roughly constructed of timber
and *without* lights from one year's end to another, with a foot of
granulated peat brought to within a few inches of the frame top.
On no account should the plants be sunk, as it is vital they should
have fresh circulating air and as much sunshine as can be given to
them. The wooden frame is just sufficient to shield the plants from
cold winds, and being in peat they are never dry. Frost in these conditions, even up to 40 degrees, does not injure them, and not a
single plant suffered in the winter of 1947. So rich a treasure is this
heath that it is well worth while going to a little trouble to provide
reasonable protection in exposed situations. The plants in the
frame are excellent specimens, they flower perfectly and abundantly
and improve after being trimmed in the spring.

Lest the reader should think that the plants are kept permanently
in a frame, I ought to explain that single ones are removed from
time to time to the private garden surrounding the house. There is
no fun merely in keeping them all in a frame. Those taken away
are given protection in various ways, among rocks in the rockery,
in a sunken bog garden where there is plenty of light and sunshine
but shelter from cold winds, some are screened by trees in the
shrubbery, and others by the taller tree heaths in the heather
garden. Copious quantities of peat fill the hole at the time of planting. These are not only the best but the safest ways of growing
successfully the *Daboëcia* heaths.

The St Dabeoc's heath grows to about two feet and has a graceful
array of long, tapering stems with vivid, glossy, dark green leaves
white underneath. The flowers along the top portion of the stem
are about half an inch long and egg-shaped and of a cheerful rose
purple—a very pleasing contrast to the fresh green foliage.

A writer in *Gardening Illustrated* dated March 1946 points out
that the white form, var. *alba*, does not seem to have attracted much
attention, although it is common in Ireland and S.W. Europe, and
was first discovered in Connemara about 1820. His comprehensive
description of the plant is well worth quoting:

'The bushes reach an eventual height of 18 inches to 24 inches,
sending up erect slender stems clothed in glandular hairs. The
leaves, paler in colour than those of the type, are from $\frac{1}{4}$ inch to
$\frac{3}{8}$ inch long, and $\frac{1}{8}$ inch to $\frac{1}{4}$ inch wide, and tapering at both

extremities. Whilst on their upper glossy surface there are only a few rare hairs, the lower side is furnished with dense down, thus making an effective contrast to the polished upper surface when a breeze ripples the foliage. During the summer months there emerges from each leaf axil a cluster of two or three small leaves. The flowers, carried in erect terminal racemes from June until November, are bell-shaped and from $\frac{1}{8}$ inch to $\frac{1}{2}$ inch in length. These hanging bells are constricted at the mouth, where there are four very small reflexed lobes. In colour, the blossoms are pure white and they are carried on $\frac{1}{4}$ inch stalks. These 3 inch to 5 inch racemes are borne at the end of the majority of branches.'

The writer of this valuable note to whom I am indebted does not disclose his name but signs himself appropriately 'Irlandais'.

D. cantabrica is an attractive shrub of sturdy upright habit, with pink flowers in fairly light soil; but the whole plant deepens its tones in both leaf and flower to a rose purple after becoming established for some years in peat.

All through the summer months the blossoms of the white form, *D. c. alba*, as described by 'Irlandais', are too numerous to count; the variety *globosa* is even better, the flowers being larger and rounder and of a pure white. The purple is inherent in the variety *atropurpurea*, which is richer and deeper than *D. cantabrica*, and is a lovely plant when in full bloom. *D. c. bicolor* is in the nature of an oddity, displaying both the purple and the white in the flower, with a trace of pink. In separate beds of white and purple plants grown for some time in peat, occasional seedlings produce both colours, and the pink tinge is more pronounced through the action or the influence of the peat. I have yet to find the variety *bicolor* as free-blooming as the others.

Some years ago the Azores plant *Daboëcia azorica* came into this country, only to suffer losses in severe winters. I remember seeing, one May morning, a fine group in full flower in the rockery at Kew, but on returning a few years later I noticed they had disappeared. Probably the 1947 winter had killed them. A dwarf plant, with rosy-crimson bells very freely produced, it should be cultivated where climatic conditions are relatively mild; it has the advantage of flowering in either late spring or early summer.

A new variety is *Praegerae*, a plant found in Connemara by Mrs Praeger. When this was shown to me by a friend I was

The Portuguese Heath, *Erica lusitanica*, with white flowers in early spring.

Left: Praegeri is one of the outstanding varieties of *Erica Tetralix*—it is a brilliant pink.

Below: Erica Tetralix Mackaiana has bright pink bells. It has been suggested that this should rank as a species.

Heathers in the garden of Eagles' Nest, Zennor, close to the Cornish coast; *Erica arborea* in the background.

A glowing cherry pink contrasting with the dark foliage characterises *Erica vagans* Mrs D. F. Maxwell.

impressed by its beautiful bells. The bud is deep pink and the large flowers pink-flushed.

Clipping well back in spring is beneficial to older plants and a little trimming helps younger ones. I find cuttings taken in August strike better in peat than in sand.

Unlike the heathers, the faded blooms do not remain on the plants throughout the winter but fall before the year's end.

Erica arborea—see Tree Heaths, p. 133.

Erica australis—see Tree Heaths, p. 135.

ERICA CANALICULATA

(Latin canaliculatus, grooved, referring to the leaves)

A plant of this species reposes in a pot on the table a foot or two away from where I am writing these notes in February. It came from Northern Ireland about a month ago and one would not risk it in the garden at this time of the year.

According to Bean it makes an evergreen bush up to 18 feet in height but is, unfortunately, not absolutely hardy. It is, however, hardier than is commonly supposed and should be planted more often, not only in Cornish gardens where specimens have been known to attain 17 feet, but also in the milder districts of Sussex, Hampshire and Dorset. A plant survived for three years at Kew some time ago, at the foot of a wall, protected by canvas. It flowered outside but eventually succumbed to a severe frost.

The pale pink-tinted flowers make it one of the most attractive of flowering shrubs for the first three months of the year. Out of flower, its graceful, columnar outline, with its small fine-pointed leaves make it an asset to any garden. It is a Cape Heath and is often confused commercially with *Erica melanthera*. The latter, another Cape Heath, is however, only one to two feet high, bearing pale or bright red flowers, with black anthers, and is probably not in cultivation in Great Britain.

ERICA CARNEA

(Latin caro, flesh, from the colour of the corolla)

As the daylight increases to brighten the New Year, the *carnea* heaths begin to bloom in warm, fresh, glowing tints of colour. They kindle the moorland scene with soft pink and rich carmine and deepest red. They challenge the coldest frost and fiercest wind, their flowers are pools of fire in melting snows. No wonder it is called the alpine forest heath or mountain heath, for it is distributed over a wide alpine chain, on heaths and in pinewoods in Italy, Austria, France and other countries at an altitude exceeding 2,000 feet above sea-level.

The higher the planting ground the better and more vigorous the growth. The severest winter causes it no injury. The entire collection of our *Erica carnea* on the Pennines was unimpaired during and following the zero frosts in the early winters of the war and also the terrible winter of 1947. All the plants were fully exposed to powerful and bitterly cold north-east winds, which ripped down certain shrubs and smashed buddleias and laurels into crumpled matchwood, the arctic gale continuing unabated for many weeks. They had to endure long periods of intensely hard frosts, reaching nearly forty degrees; for two months we did not see them, for they lay gripped in ice and snow. It is as well to bear in mind that unlike most other plants in the garden, they were in bud just before the onslaught, but when the thaw came the brave little heaths were seen again and emerged smiling in the spring dawn with all their fresh and lovely blooms unspoiled as though there had been no winter at all.

Frankly, I have not experienced anything quite like this before, and it goes to prove that these early-flowering heaths are unique in the plant world; no matter how vile the weather may be, nothing prevents them from flowering successfully. Putting it another way, their flowering life is entirely independent of the season's conditions.

Without wishing to be dogmatic, I think I am right in saying that no hardier plant exists in the wide field of garden cultivation: one could grow *E. carnea* to flower perfectly on the slopes of Ben Nevis or on the summit of Snowdon. Indeed, the more open the situation of pure mountain air the sturdier it becomes, the quicker the buds develop to maturity, the sooner the flower appears, and the richer in colour when it comes. The carneas of our garden never flowered better than in the spring which followed the abnormal winter already described.

Several hundreds clothe part of the moorland within the northern boundary of the house; they are free from the shadows of trees,

buildings, and walls which cut down the full measure of light from
sun and sky. There are others in a more sheltered part of the garden
facing south where shadows fall. The former are in bloom *nearly
a month* earlier than the latter, yet the distance between one group
of plants (north) and the other (south) is no more than 200 yards.

To say that *carnea* heaths grow almost anywhere is a broad
statement to make, and there is one excepted situation, that of
industrial towns and cities in which the smoky atmosphere is
injurious to heaths and heathers alike. Nevertheless, carneas are
known to be quite happy even near to industry, as, for example, in
parts of south Lancashire, where they are successfully cultivated in
public parks and private gardens. In and around other provincial
towns, outside the industrial belt, and in London parks they do
well. It is, in fact, a most accommodating plant in many varied
situations of the British Isles, requiring only the attention of a little
trimming to keep it tidy in the course of many years' development.

Adaptable to ordinary garden soil, it prospers in lime, and
readers who are fond of heathers but have been unable to grow
them because of chalk in their soil will find the *carnea* just as happy
in lime as it is anywhere else. If the ground is on the heavy side
and deep in stodgy clay, it is better to dig the stuff out and sub-
stitute rotted loam for preference, but should loam not be available
then ordinary garden soil will suffice. On the other hand, where clay
can be broken up it should be mixed with well-forked friable soil
which is what carneas enjoy. Sandy soil needs granulated peat
worked into it, and top-dressed as well as worked again with peat
in the spring. In other than a light sandy soil, peat is not essential,
but a sprinkling of lime occasionally is beneficial.

Propagate by layering, as described in the chapter on Propaga-
tion, or cuttings in open ground on a wet August day. Roots may
be pulled out from side pieces of old plants and replanted. Very
old plants become ungainly and, when dug up for the purpose of
making divisions, flop into a tangled mass almost beyond control.
I have found it is better to cut back the foliage to within a few
inches of the ground before lifting these old plants: divisions can
then be made more readily.

Flower buds formed in the summer (July and August) make such
rapid expansion that one naturally imagines the plants will flower
and fade long before Christmas. When you come to think of it,
nine months is a fair stretch of time from the birth of the bud to

the passing of the flower, but that is the floral life of each season's carneas—mid-July to mid-April. The flowers are large and prolific in numbers compared with the dwarf size of the plant—six to nine inches. Probably no other plant of similar size produces anything like the quantity of blooms as are to be found on a full-grown carnea. I defy anyone to count the number.

Pleasing to the eye is the shade variation in the foliage; James Backhouse, for example, is a lovely deep shining green, so also is Springwood, while Pink Pearl and Prince of Wales are lighter, in contrast to the bronze *Vivellii*. Then in May and June the new foliage which reclothes the plants is so fresh and charming that it makes a valuable contribution to the summer garden.

The leaves are very fine and narrow, invariably in fours, about a third of an inch long with a blend of tints, in pale green, deep green, greyish green, to lighter shades including streaks of yellow. Flowers appear singly and in pairs in the leaf axils of the previous summer's growth; both the anthers and corolla are red, the latter about half an inch, and the calyx more than half the length of the corolla.

When the qualities of both flower and foliage are combined, the *carnea* heath is of outstanding garden merit, and enthusiasts are never tired of telling how indispensable it is to the heather garden. One would go further and say it is indispensable to any garden.

Another feature of the whole of the *carnea* group is the picturesque downward trend of the bells, which are tightly clustered on each stem, a feature all the more effective when the plants are in a slightly elevated position, on a sloping rockery, or a bank, or a rising moorland.

These delightful prostrate sprawling heaths (each one as it matures covers three to four feet of space) have received many labels in the course of hybridisation. Some are named after nursery firms who introduced them into our gardens, Backhouse and Beale; some bear royal titles, Prince of Wales and Queen Mary; some are named appropriately to colour, Ruby Glow and Pink Pearl; some include the seasons in their names, Winter Beauty and Springwood; and in some there is poetry—*gracilis, praecox rubra* and Queen of Spain.

We owe a tremendous debt to the well-known house of Back-house of York, who pioneered many of those beautiful heaths on the commercial market. They brought out many forms and gave appropriate titles to the various varieties. The true native that bears only the name *carnea* is bright rosy pink, to which a whole string of appendages has been attached.

There are nearly thirty named varieties, some so much alike that only a botanical student, or a man who has spent a lifetime in a heather nursery, can tell one from the other. When they are out of bloom it is more difficult still, but certain distinguishing features in the foliage serve as a clue for identification. For example, Winter Beauty and King George certainly go together; so do Prince of Wales and Pink Pearl. As they are practically identical there would appear to be no need for four names. Two are quite sufficient, and those of us who are born with an inherent enthusiasm for royalty might prefer to retain the royal titles. But I like the name of Winter Beauty which fits the plant as perfectly as any name could do.

Perhaps too many names are given to these pictureque and somewhat modest plants, for modest they are, compared with chrysanthemums, geraniums, and the like. Fewer names would serve the purpose equally well, but whatever we choose to call them there can never be and there certainly never are too many flowers among the carneas!

VARIETIES OF ERICA CARNEA

alba   January-April

For many years the only white *carnea* cultivated, a dull thing, unworthy of the species, now fortunately superseded by two greatly improved forms, Cecilia M. Beale and Springwood White. It filled the gap until the better ones came along—that is all one can say for it. *Carnea* plants as a whole are so much to be appreciated that one hesitates to criticise adversely this old variety; but it has no future.

atrorubra   March-April

Like the scene painter who applies the final coat of paint to the scenery before the show begins, so this heath puts the finishing touches to the long succession of blooms for which the carneas are noted. It is one of the last to flower, and what *c. gracilis* is to the winter season so *atrorubra* is to the spring. The long spikes are a deep rich crimson, the foliage is of a glaucous shade, and it makes a fine combination with a group of daffodils. (The carneas always look well as carpeters to spring-flowering plants and shrubs.) There have been many new varieties since *atrorubra* came into the market, but I could never see my way clear to abandon this attractive and trustworthy plant.

C. J. Backhouse
March-April

Another late variety, in direct contrast to *atrorubra*, and a very pale pink, probably the palest of all the carneas. It comes into bud as a faint wash. The blooms appear on intermittent little columns, in clusters up the stem, a peculiar, uncommon effect. Examine the buds closely and you will see minute breaks, and, after a break, there is a larger cluster of buds as though making up for those missing in the gap. This is a habit all its own.

carnea
January-April

No, it is not a misprint, for this is *Erica carnea carnea*, a very old friend indeed. Quite apart from the pink blossoms so welcome in the New Year, the character of the plant is worthy of its thrice-blessed name. The leaves are a vivid green; it is sturdy, compact, fascinating and essential to the scheme of things. I am reminded of an incident of some years ago, during a visit to a nursery when I took a friend to see the carneas in January. Both he and I became dizzy at the sight of so many varieties and so many names! Finally, after a grand tour of reviewing a comprehensive collection we came to an exceptionally large plant in a show border and agreed it was about the finest we had seen. Then the following conversation took place between us and the foreman:

'What is the name of this one?'

'Carnea.'

'Yes, we know that—but the name of the variety?'

'Carnea,' he reaffirmed.

Then it dawned on me—there was *Erica carnea carnea*, brilliantly displaying hundreds of magnificent pink blossoms. Without doubt that was the finest *carnea* heath I had ever seen and I could not wish to have come across a better plant anywhere.

Cecilia M. Beale
January-March

As the New Year dawns the buds of gracilis and others are opening, to be followed by the first white, Cecilia M. Beale. Its habit is different from its companion, Springwood, which begins to flower in February, being dwarf and compact, and for its size it bears large blooms. This is all the more interesting because the spikes are not long and although they are fairly close to the ground the bloom is not spoilt by foul weather. The value of this heath is that it is an early white.

Eileen Porter   December-April

A new variety flowering as early as October in some parts of the country, but the plants I have seen in a northern garden were later. As the flowers, of carmine shade, are said to be in bloom longer than any other variety it must be a remarkable *carnea*. I have not had sufficient experience of the plant to express an opinion.

gracilis   December-March

Grown here for more years than I can remember, a favourite heather of mine, one of the oldest and one of the best. The earliest pink, a lovely plant in masses in a large bed. The foliage is minute, the plant very dwarf and of neat habit. Winter time always seems to be brighter by the presence of this rich pink heath.

James Backhouse   March-April

Has the largest blooms of all the carneas. Foliage is a good green; it is green in the bud, the flower a sweet soft pink in the spring. One of the finest of the Backhouse varieties, if not one of the best of heathers.

King George   March-April

Among the few carneas to receive distinction by the R.H.S., it has gained an Award of Merit. Those who have grown the plant will agree how well it has earned such honours, for in every heather garden it has a recognised place, in fact, no heather garden is complete without it. A very beautiful plant, laden with deep rosy-crimson flowers.

Loughrigg   February-March

As a new variety it has only recently been planted in our garden. I notice the pleasing combination of glaucous blue-green foliage and light green turning to bronze at the tips and the flowers are a rich purple.

Mrs Sam Doncaster   January-April

Comes next to James Backhouse in robustness, although it is softer in habit and not as strong in stem. An ideal carpeter, and flowers early with light pink blooms.

pallida   March-April

Pale pink, not as well known and not seen as often as it should be in our gardens. Quite a good plant.

Pink Pearl or Pink Beauty   March-April

Light green foliage and shell-pink flowers. It truly is a pearl, as its name implies. Late blooming and a very pretty plant.

praecox rubra   January-March

Similar to Queen of Spain. A touch of red is marked in the bud, and the flowers, rather on the small size, are a deep, rich red. A popular *carnea* heath, it should have a place in the rockery.

Prince of Wales   March-April

Begins to flower when the winter varieties are fading. One of the latest, it has never bloomed as freely with me as many others have; but I admire the plant for its distinctive foliage, which is loose and elegant and more open than the carpeters. I have seen it still a charming pink shade when Whitsuntide has been in May.

Queen Mary   December-February

Is this the first *carnea* to bloom? The new variety, Eileen Porter, may now precede it. I write these lines on December 17, 1949, and looking round the garden this morning I find some plants of this variety are in flower as well as *gracilis* and Winter Beauty. They run each other so close that one would have to be up at dawn to see which popped out of bud first. In some years Queen Mary is in full bloom at Christmas. It is a good rich pink, a true type of *carnea*, which seems to be better in some seasons than others. On certain soils it hardly flowers at all.

There must be a reason for these fluctuating changes. I think it is more reliable on lime than peat, for the leaves are liable to turn to a lightish green shade which is almost golden in acid ground. I have noticed that young plants bear little evidence of this variation, it is when they are older that the acidity asserts itself so as to change the appearance considerably. This rather unnatural hue is conspicuous in plants of mature age grown in deep, strong peat. It can be remedied by a lime dressing.

Queen of Spain   March-April

An open plant, which means fewer branches and more freedom in habit than the compact carpeters, and distinguished by a light shining leaf, about twice as large as that of *Vivellii*. Can be picked out easily in a batch of carneas by the lightness of its foliage. It is of interest to observe that the fin of the leaf points downwards, which is unusual as the fins of the other plants are either horizontal or turning upwards. There is a touch of red in the bud and the late flowers are a pleasing light pink.

Rosy Gem   March-April

One of the few carneas not in my collection, nor have I seen a plant anywhere. There is also another, *c. rosea*, which is unfamiliar to me. I understand both are well worth growing, the former bells of a gay pink, the latter a paler shade.

Ruby Glow   March-April

My opinion of this plant is very high. The blooms are true to its name, a rich ruby colour, an improvement on *atrorubens* and a brighter red than *Vivellii*.

Snow Queen   January-March

This plant has been praised by some and decried by others. The description given to it of large white flowers does not bear out what I saw of some plants in a north-country nursery, where they were considered disappointing. The plant appeared to be reliable in young stages and until it became a fair size; then the whole thing partly disintegrated and the blooms became smaller and sparser. Peaty soil may have been responsible for the failure, and it is probably a better plant in the south than the north.

Springwood   February-April

Better judges than the writer have placed this heath in the first six of all the heathers—nearly 200—under cultivation. Each of its all-round qualities is superb: there is a brilliant freshness, a vivid green, about the foliage. The large pure white and pink flowers smother the long and plentiful spikes and the yield of bloom in a well-established plant is enormous. So capacious is Springwood that it will easily cover two to three feet of space and never look untidy or get out of hand. The more it grows the better it looks. Buds are tinged yellow (in the crimson-flowering varieties, a paler or greenish-yellow), the blossoms rimmed with chocolate-coloured anthers—a minute fringe over a dead white surface.

I make bold to say that Springwood is the fastest-growing heather we have; the *Calluna* variety, *Alportii*, is a close rival. To raise stock by tiny cuttings in pots of sand and peat is a mere waste of time, for all one need do is to lift a plant and put it down a little deeper, not too deep, with young growing tips peeping above the surface. As long as the plant is not wholly buried it will not rot. The number of young plants which will root in twelve months' time is surprisingly large, and I know a nursery which raised 10,000 in so short a time in one bed alone. Layering according to the method described on page 54 will produce even more plants.

The pink form is comparatively new and appeared as a seedling in a Scottish garden. It is every bit as good as the white, which was found in Italy. The latter was given an Award of Merit by the R.H.S. in 1930.

Throughout the whole year Springwood retains its bright green leaves. I have seen it in the course of a prolonged summer heatwave as fresh as if there had been rain all night, when other totally different types of plant were so parched they had to be continually watered to keep them alive.

Thomas Kingscote
March-April

Spring flowering, pale pink, one of the many fine carneas introduced by the house of Backhouse.

Urville
February-March

A short while ago I received a plant of this variety from a Cheshire nursery. It has very deep green foliage, probably darker than *Vivellii*, and rose-pink flowers.

Vivellii
February-March

An unusual type of *carnea*, quite different from all the others. A well-known nursery firm in Northern Ireland regard it as the best of the lot. The foliage changes with the seasons, from dark green during the summer months to a red shade in the winter, when the bronze buds appear, before breaking into a rich carmine-red bell.

Winter Beauty
December-March

Although the last in the alphabet it deserves to be on top. Always welcome because it never fails to flower at Christmas; if the weather is mild the bloom begins in November, and the plant is at its best in the New Year. The rich deep pink bells have been well described as "winter cheer".

GALL MIDGES

A writer in *Cheshire Life* states that he found a comparatively unknown pest on certain *carnea* beds in a Yorkshire garden. He noticed that almost every shoot, particularly of the variety *Vivellii*, which was planted in drifts, terminated in a tuft, which proved to be a gall containing a reddish larva. Specimens were submitted to Dr H. F. Barnes of Rothamsted, the world authority on gall midges, who identified the pest as *Wachtliella ericina*, and kindly supplied the information that it had only been reported previously in 1946 and 1947. So far no other species of heath has been attacked, but it is believed that all varieties of *E. carnea* are susceptible. Control measures are so far unknown (concludes the writer), but hand-picking and destroying the galls during the winter is recommended, though this is not practicable where large quantities are grown.

The tuft referred to, in this magazine contribution, is not new to me, as I have noticed it for some years among my carneas, particularly with the varieties *gracilis* and *praecox rubra*. Not all are affected, as the swelling develops in size towards the end of autumn and recedes after hard frosts have killed off so much of the midge life. No other part of the stem is attacked in this way, nor does the plant show any signs of distress. Its robust nature remains and the flowers appear as usual. Up to now I have found it nothing to worry about.

ERICA CINEREA

(*Latin* cinis, *ashes, from the grey colour*)

This is the Scotch or Grey Heath, sometimes described as the Fine-leaved or Twisted Heath, though most of us know it better by the familiar name of Bell Heather. It is a native of our British Isles and in many parts runs riot, on the moors in Devon, Cornwall and Somerset, over the Highlands of Scotland and mountains of Wales, and on the west coast of the Isle of Man, where it competes against the strong growth of the true heather (*Calluna*) for the survival of the fittest. One often finds the purple bells mingling with the late-flowering gorse (*Ulex europaeus*), sprouting through the yellow spines in picturesque irregular clumps. Have you ever tried to lift one out of the gorse?

The *cinerea* heath has a neat, well-proportioned shape, and never seems to get out of hand, the stiff and slender branches (which easily break) growing from six inches to a foot. The very fine, smooth, linear leaves, about ¼ inch long, are a deep green, usually in whorls of three. The flowers of the native type are purple, but they vary in colour among those which have been cultivated. Their numbers, by no means uniform, can be as many as eight as they appear in terminal umbels. The corolla is egg-shaped, $\frac{1}{4}$ inch long, the calyx shorter.

The heights of the plants, some quite diminutive and others resembling a nicely-shaped bush, are no less conspicuous than the pleasing and interesting contrasts in flower colours and number of blooms.

That they are sun lovers goes without saying, for when the summer sunshine beats down day after day over vast stretches of moorland country where there is little shade above the plants but copious depths of peat below them, the bell heathers are in full bloom. In a garden of dry and sandy soil they should be given liberal dressings of granulated peat at regular intervals and the roots must be throughly soaked with this compost. They enjoy pure air, mist and dew, a cool moist soil, and sunshine. It is important to see that the ground is well drained, for they will not stand waterlogged conditions.

Most of the many varieties of *cinerea* introduced into commerce have been excellent plants, while one or two have not quite come up to expectations. I do not choose to condemn a particular plant because it has failed in one's garden or because it does not appear precisely as the nurseryman described it in his catalogue. It is not so much a matter of opinion on the face value of a plant as seen or read about as one of experience in growing it upon which true opinion is ultimately based. If there are varieties among the cinereas which have yet to be as successful as other heaths and heathers, then I am not putting the blame on the plants. It would be wrong to do so, for the trouble might well be a local one of soil or climate; it might be anything.

VARIETIES OF ERICA CINEREA

alba   June-August   9 *inches*

Some growers seem disappointed because in their opinion the *cinerea* has not produced a white form comparable with *mediterranea* W. T. Rackliff, *carnea* Springwood and *vagans* Lyonesse. But I frankly think that *cinerea alba* is a splendid plant and I would not do without it. Probably the best of the *cinerea* whites, the long spikes provide plenty of bloom amid the apple-green foliage. Even when out of flower, as I have seen it this morning in mid-January, it is an attractive plant.

alba major   June-August   9 *inches*
Rather different from and does not bloom as freely as *alba*. The flowers appear in limited numbers at the stem ends.

alba minor   June-August   6 *inches*
Both this and the *major* are delightful little plants, very neat and compact, the former not exceeding nine inches in its rich green foliage. *Alba* is more open than the other two which are dense in habit.

Apple Blossom   June-August   1 *foot*
Whitish blossoms with a flush of delicate shell-pink well clothe this lovely *cinerea*. It is not as hardy as one would like it to be in certain northern gardens; older plants are slow to recover and some deteriorate after a hard winter. A young plant, well grown in a warm and sheltered spot, is as sweet an object as one could wish to see anywhere.

atropurpurea   July-August   1 *foot*
Here we have another plant not as vigorous as *alba*; some seasons it hardly seems to grow at all. The flowers are a much brighter purple than the bell heather of the moors, and for this reason alone its name suits it well.

atrorubens   July-August   6 *inches*
One of the finest cinereas, with long sprays of abundant ruby red flowers. It should always be included in the heather garden.

atrosanguinea   July-August   6 *inches*
Two varieties are listed, one named Reuthe's, a darkish red, and the other, Smith's, dark scarlet. The latter, which I grow, is a rich colour, a brilliant, showy plant in July.

carnea   July-August   1 *foot*
A pink shade, not as well known as the others.

C. D. Eason   June-July   9 *inches*
An outstanding plant, of bright red flowers and deep green foliage. Makes quite a shapely little bush.

C. G. Best   June-July   1 *foot*
A valuable addition to the species. Grows with me to about a foot,

has a well-defined shape, and long spikes of a strong salmon pink, which stand out against the dark green leaves. Its characteristics are uncommon for the general type of *cinerea* heath.

coccinea (Smith's variety)   June-August   3-4 *inches*
One of the smallest and as a dwarf heath has only a few rivals. It is so prostrate as to be mere inches above the soil, and as I have a group of about two dozen, their size is in the nature of a curiosity. The flowers are a deep carmine red, and so intense is the colour of the bells that one blinks when looking at them in strong sunlight. Considering the lilliputian stature, it is one of the most remarkable of heaths cultivated. Some of the plants sold, and even those exhibited at flower shows are not always true to the *coccinea* depth of colour, but Smith's variety is always reliable.

Domino   June-July   9 *inches*
Dark green foliage and white flowers with tiny black anthers so minute that they appear like specks of dust. You have to look closely at the flower stalks to see them. The plant came to me recently from a nursery where I saw a number in bloom, and the description given to it was, I thought, rather exaggerated. It is said to have ebony stalks, but I failed to see a true ebony colour in them—the shade was just a dull brown. One feature I noticed was the large number of flowers.

Eden Valley   June-July   .   6 *inches*
A splendid new plant, light green leaves and lilac-pink flowers; the pink fades gradually as the lower part of the bell is white.

Francis   June-July   1 *foot*
This is a very good *cinerea*, which has no alliance with Domino nor has it any trace of purple. The flowers are a bright cerise, the foliage bronze.

Golden Drop   June-July   4 *inches*
So modest is this plant that it has almost forgotten how to bloom in our garden. After some years it produced one pink flower, and perhaps next summer there will be two. To describe it as shy is to trifle with words. But the foliage amply makes up for the absence of blossom as the plant forms a dense mat of copper to gold colour and so deep a red does it become in the winter that by the time March comes round one begins to imagine the plant is passing out.

Then in the spring it breaks into fresh life and the leaves revert to copper and gold. I regard it as a first-class foliage plant.

Golden Hue   June-July   1 *foot*
A foliage plant, similar to the last, but more golden.

G. Osmond   June-July   1 *foot*
I have not had this plant long enough to form an opinion but it impressed me when I first saw it, with very pale purple flowers.

John Eason   June-July   1 *foot*
Golden foliage and pink flowers which deepen as they mature—a plant of charming contrasts.

Knap Hill Variety   July-August   1 *foot*
Long pink sprays, neat olive-green foliage and a fine dwarf habit. Should be grown more than it is and although not always listed in the catalogues nurserymen usually supply it upon request.

lilacina   June-July   1 *foot*
One cannot write too highly of this beautiful *cinerea*. The foliage, light green and attractive in midwinter as well as in summer, affords high relief to the delicate shade of lilac in the bells. I do not know where this plant came from or who first discovered or raised it, but it is a real gem.

Mrs Dill   June-July   4 *inches*
Only a few inches high, a choice dwarf, with a spreading habit and bright pink flowers.

pallida   June-August   6 *inches*
A smallish plant, of pale purple.

P. S. Patrick   June-July   1 *foot*
As the name indicates, an Irish variety, sturdy in growth and very hardy, quite unlike the usual type. It sends up long spikes of rich, large, purple flowers, in a succession of bloom for ten weeks. This is a plant highly recommended, deserving all the nice things said about it. Grows freely with me in an open situation and came through the winter of 1947 uninjured.

purpurea   July-September   1 *foot*
The purple bell heather of our countryside brought under cultivation. I have a number in the garden which do well as long as there is liberal moisture at the roots.

pygmaea   June-July   6 *inches*
Four to six inches, a good dwarf; pink flowers.

rosea   June-August   1 *foot*
One of the oldest of varieties, it has not as yet been pushed out by newer and somewhat novel rivals. That it has held its own against so many speaks well for its traditional virtues. *Rosea* is a very easy plant to cultivate, robust, hardy, and soon spreading into a mat of dense foliage combined with plenty of clear rose bells which look so bright and cheerful.

Rosabella   June-August   6-9 *inches*
A plant of dense foliage, with pink flowers.

Rose Queen   June-July   1 *foot*
Like *rosea* hardly a day passes in summer when it is not in bloom, and it also has a matted habit. The leaves are a fresh green, the flowers in abundance of rose-pink. An excellent plant in every way.

Ruby   June-July   6 *inches*
A purple form blended with ruby.

Startler   June-July   6 *inches*
Fresh green leaves, beautifully spaced along the stems, a most attractive plant, dwarf and neat, with deep, glowing, pink flowers.

spicata   June-July   6 *inches*
A pretty little plant, with pale lilac bells on the small side.

schizopetala   June-July   1 *foot*
The petals are split, and the flowers a pale purple, with green leaves fringed with bronze.

splendens   June-July   1 *foot*
Deep rose flowers.

Victoria   June-July   1 *foot*
A good plant, of large, rosy purple blooms. So strong is the colour that it is one of the best of the purple cinereas.

ERICA CILIARIS

(*Latin* cilium, *an eye-lash, from the leaves fringed with hairs*)
In the flowering sequence following the cinereas is the Dorset

Lyonesse is an outstanding white variety of *Erica vagans*.

Like Lyonesse, the pink St Keverne has received an Award of Merit.

George Rendall is a winter- and spring-flowering hybrid with purple flowers.

Erica darleyensis, a reddish flowered hybrid between *E. mediterranea* and *E. carnea*.

The tiny flowers of the hybrid W. G. Notley— a cross between *Erica cinerea* and *Calluna vulgaris*—are exceptional among the heathers.

H. Maxwell, a hybrid of *Erica ciliaris* and *E. Tetralix,* bears its large pink blossoms over four summer months.

A mass of *Erica carnea Vivellii* with *Erica arborea alpina* in the background.

Heath, *E. ciliaris*, which varies in height from six inches to a foot in its native ground and does not exceed two feet in the varieties. It is trailing in habit, unfolding small, oval-shaped hairy leaves, which are a trifle sticky, in whorls of three on fine slender stalks; the leaves, about $\frac{1}{8}$ inch long, green above and white underneath, are slightly turned under at the edges. The foliage alone distinguishes it from other species, being a pale green.

Its main features are the exquisite tones of the flowers where clear pink and rich rosy shades predominate, as distinct from bell heathers generally in which purple prevails. Bearing in mind that the number of varieties is limited, compared, say, with the carneas and cinereas, the floral contribution of the Dorset heath is remarkably good in the heather garden. There are no nondescripts among its varieties.

Bloom begins in June and continues until October; even in January one observes the faded russet corollas. The flowers face one way in whorls of threes on terminal racemes and in one or two of the stronger varieties there are as many as four clustered at the terminals. The egg-shaped, inverted bells, about half an inch long, overcrowd the restricted length of the three to five inches of the racemes. It will be noticed that the corolla is rosy-red, pitcher-shaped, and contracted at the mouth.

Those blooms which appear first fade out and are brown before the succeeding top buds break into blossom, and the two combined, the flower in full splendour above and the faded one below, enhance the charming contrasts of the plant. *Ciliaris* should be grown in soil that is not of a calcareous nature. It enjoys moist ground and full sunshine. In many south-country gardens it has given every satisfaction, but where smoke and fog pollute the atmosphere, round London, for example, it may be short-lived. In some other parts of the country the Dorset heath is inclined to be uncertain and, although looking rather sick with us after a severe winter, it soon recovers in the warmer spring days. Extreme weather has never killed this heath in our garden.

VARIETIES OF ERICA CILIARIS

alba   July-August   1 *foot*
Small flowers, plentiful, the first of the *ciliaris* whites to be grown, now much improved upon by the newer introduction, Stoborough.

aurea   July-August   1 *foot*

This pretty-looking plant, like some of the other golden-foliage varieties of heaths and heathers, is not free flowering nor as robust. The leaves afford an uncommon break from the type.

globosa   July-October   18 *inches*

A splendid Dorset heath, vigorous and hardy, growing into a midget bush. The umbels are clustered with large pink bells for well over three months and they are just as rich in autumn as in summer.

hybrida   June-October   6 *inches*

Outrivals *globosa* in a long period of bloom. I have seen it in full flower while the days are still lengthening in June and a few odd blossoms appearing from the same plant at the beginning of November. A compact dwarf, with bright yellow tips at the shoots in the spring when it is an attractive foliage plant; the flowers are rosy-pink. Other hybrids between *ciliaris* and *Tetralix* are similar in their golden tips in spring and early summer.

Maweana   June-October   1 *foot*

Mr George Maw discovered this plant in Portugal as far back as 1872. It is of stronger growth than the average *ciliaris* heath, the stems are more rigid and upright in habit, the pink flowers larger.

Mrs C. H. Gill   July-October   1 *foot*

Of outstanding merit, the small dark green leaves contrasting with the rich red flowers, of which there are many. One of the best varieties, as the strong red is conspicuous among the pinks.

rotundifolia   July-October   1 *foot*

A pink form which I have grown for many years. Looks well in a rockery.

Stoborough   July-October   2 *feet*

I regard this plant as the most vigorous of the species and hardy enough to resist without injury our hardest winters. The tallest *ciliaris* and the strongest in growth, its pitcher-shaped, pearly white flowers are larger than the type and freely borne. As good a white heath as one could wish for, an ideal plant which I recommend whole-heartedly.

Wych   July-October   18 *inches*

Light pink flowers, long spikes, and many blooms.

Erica codonodes—see under Tree Heaths, p. 135.

Erica lusitanica—see under Tree Heaths, p. 135.

ERICA MEDITERRANEA

(*Latin* mediterraneus, *inland remote from the sea. Opposite to* maritimus)

The shrub which was first given this title grows from six to ten feet in height, but the varieties since introduced to our gardens vary up to two feet. I am not at all sure whether the dwarfer ones should ever have been included in the true *mediterranea* species or classified instead as hybrids. In the R.H.S. book, *Some Good Garden Plants* (1922-45) it is stated: 'A hybrid that appeared in James Smith's Heath Nursery in Darley Dale was widely distributed under the name *Erica mediterannea hybrida*; it has been renamed *Erica × darleyensis*.' If this can be done with our old friend, *darleyensis*, then one or two of the *mediterranea* varieties might be regarded as hybrids, for there is a wide difference between *superba* and *m*. W. T. Rackcliff.

The *mediterranea* heath is a dense, bushy shrub; the branches, though erect in the taller forms, are of a brittle nature, and easily broken under pressure of ice and snow and by severe summer thunderstorms. The linear leaves are set in whorls of four, about $\frac{1}{3}$ of an inch long, and while the true or original shrub is a dark green colour, the shade varies in some varieties.

Buds are formed in the autumn for the coming spring blooms, of which there are many, the flowers, singly or in pairs, appearing in the leaf axils; the racemes several inches long are on the previous year's growth. The corolla is a rich rose crimson, the anthers dark red, and when in full bloom the shrub pervades the garden with a fragrance that is deliciously sweet.

During the war years of double summertime it was my practice in the spring, when there is more to do out of doors than at any other season, to be working in the garden at six o'clock in the morning. True Greenwich time was, of course, 4 a.m. and often on an early April morning a heavy dew caused by moorland mist covered the plants. The delicate honey-like odour which came from the *mediterranea* heaths and a bed of over 200 *hybrida darleyensis* was indescribably beautiful. Three hours later, when the dew had evaporated and the mists rolled away in the bright morning sunshine, the fragrance was no more.

These glorious spring plants are a valuable contribution to the heather garden, as a link in the flowering sequence of the two seasons winter and summer. They begin to show blossom as the carneas fade and continue to bloom until the early cinereas break from the bud. Hardier than the tree heaths, they are nothing like as dependable as the carneas, and one or two varieties suffer much damage in very cold, exposed places and all of them are uncertain of survival when the mercury is down to zero.

Although they have come through without loss with me, as mentioned elsewhere in this book, it is advisable to give them some form of protection where you can and a south-west aspect, if possible. So much the better if there are fences or walls, hedges and trees (beech, for example) and a shrubbery, to serve as a windbreak from the cutting early spring winds when the plants are advanced in bud or just beginning to flower.

As I have never been able to provide adequate shelter on the north and east side of our one-acre garden, a precautionary measure was taken when the first *mediterranea* heaths were planted, some years ago. I gave some of them what Dean Hole once described as 'a winter overcoat'. They were packed all round with peat in layers several inches deep (according to the height of the plant); only the tops were visible. Bracken stored in a potting shed until required was placed over the tops, of the plants, the ends of the foliage being held down by a fairly large stone to prevent the bracken from blowing away. By this method the plants were kept snug and immune from the havoc which a long and hard winter on the Pennines can create. When the air was warm with spring sunshine the trappings were removed and the flowers appeared in April as perfect as one would wish. Such precautions may seem rather elaborate but they were applied at the outset because I was uncertain as to how the *mediterranea* heaths would stand up to a really bad winter. As they have done far better than I ever imagined the packing method has long been abandoned. I mention the idea mainly as a tip to those who wish to grow these plants in conditions similar to my own.

These heaths are quite happy in most soils, particularly if they are well drained and not too heavy. Loam, peat, lime—it makes no difference. On loam here they are just as fine as in the peat beds of heather nurseries, and I have come across them flourishing on limestone. They should be grown in an open sunny situation facing south or south-west for preference, given some shelter, as already mentioned, and spacing between plants should be on the generous side.

VARIETIES OF ERICA MEDITERRANEA

alba　　　　　　March-May　　　　　　*2 feet*

A delightful rounded little shrub, cheerful at all seasons, but never so bright as in the spring when the rich green foliage is seen at its best and the flowers of pure white almost cover the plant, so many are the blooms. I remember planting *alba* about ten years ago and that single specimen looks as neat and fresh now as though it had been planted yesterday. It will always do you well, and for the modest cost in a nurseryman's list it is as sound an investment as the Bank of England. It will return the outlay in floral dividends too numerous to count. It will give no trouble, call for no attention, and I know from long experience that it never fails to please in foliage and flower alike. To the spring calendar of flowers it is a valuable contributor, and although the newer white W. T. Rackcliff produces larger blooms, and is considered a better plant, I still like the older form, a bushy shrublet of some two feet in stature.

Brightness　　　　　March-May　　　　　*2 feet*

One of the few but exceptionally good heath plants which have come to us from Ireland in recent years. Rarely more than a couple of feet tall as a bush of symmetrical charm, the foliage is deeper and the flower quite different from the type. Again, unlike other varieties, the leaves are not uniform in size, those near the top of the shrub being much smaller and far more numerous. The buds are close to the terminals in short clusters giving an appearance of overcrowding, and they are marked in strong bronze colour. These features contrast in harmony with the clear bright red flowers from which the shrub so aptly derives and so well deserves its name.

coccinea　　　　　March-May　　　　　*2 feet*

I have not seen this plant, but I understand it is like Brightness, the flowers being darker and a brighter red.

hibernica (syn. **glauca**)　March-May　　　　*3-4 feet*

Rarely exceeding four feet in height in this country, it can be distinguished by blue-green leaves, hence the synonymous name of

glauca. It does not bloom anything like as freely as the majority of
heaths, though the flowers increase in number after a fairly mild
winter, and are so pale a pink as to give one the impression that
much of the colour has been washed away by heavy rain. It is of
interest to observe the very deep purple anthers. Dr Robert Lloyd
Praeger, in his book *The Botanist in Ireland*, says that it has a
fairly wide range in the great Galway-Mayo bog area extending
from Urrisbeg (where it was first found by J. T. Mackay in
1830) near Roundstone northward at intervals to the Mullet and
Lough Conn, growing best where the peat is well drained. He adds:
'Usually forms scrubby rounded bushes about two feet in height,
easily picked out from among the other heaths by the erect twigs
and spreading leaves.' In Ireland it often commences to flower in
January and is at its best in April.

nana   March-April   18 *inches*
The dwarfest of the *mediterranea* heaths (18 inches), it has two
forms, a pink and a white known as *nana alba*. A good subject for
a rockery.

rosea   March-May   18 *inches*
Said to have some alliance with Brightness, but the flowers instead
of being a bright red are pink. It has never grown more than 18 inches
with me, and there are times when I confuse it with *rubra*.

rubra   March-May   2 *feet*
There is no pink about this one, as the blooms display a fine ruby
colour. It has the advantage of continuing to flower till June, when
the heather garden is subdued in blossom.

Silberschmeize   March-May   1 *foot*
Known as the Silver Beads heath on account of its silvery-white
flowers which are freely displayed as late as May. A small bush; a
plant that has recently reached me looks promising.

superba   March-May   4-6 *feet*
For density of growth combining both foliage and flower there is
probably no other heath to compare with this one. I doubt whether
any of the tree varieties produces the quantity of bloom of a well-
grown and well-established *superba*. It does not exceed four feet in
height with me although it grows another two feet and even more

in warmer parts of the country. The leaves, set in whorls of four, are a deep green, and when the shrub is in full bud in the New Year it has a much lighter appearance viewed as a whole than the leaf shows when examined closely. Flower buds are a pale yellow, with a touch of green, emerging from the leaf axils in tight clusters right up to the very tip of the stem. Not only are the main stems packed with flower but every one of the considerable number of side shoots is laden with blossom. Each part of the new growth bears a rich harvest of rosy-pink flowers.

Choose a spot for this shrub where it can be seen from all angles—give it a prominent place not only in the heather garden but in the shrubbery or border. It is worth growing as a single specimen shrub.

W. T. Rackliff   March-April   *2 feet.*
A splendid compact heath, strong in growth and hardy in constitution. Produces numerous large pure white flowers close to and at the tips of yellowish-green stem ends. Ranks high as a white heath.

E. melanthera—see *E. canaliculata*, p. 103.

ERICA MULTIFLORA

(*Latin* multus, *much and* flos, *a flower, many-flowered*)

A plant with which I am not familiar and one which has become rare in this country since it was introduced in 1731. It has been established at Kew, but I have not come across it there. Mr W. J. Bean in *Trees and Shrubs for English Gardens* has some interesting notes on *E. multiflora*: 'This belongs to the same type of heath as *E. vagans*, the Cornish Heath, but differs in its more compact growth and shorter racemes of flowers. Although not so vigorous and showy, it may still be preferred for some situations. It is a neater plant, and its lower branches have not the same tendency to get sprawling and ungainly as *E. vagans*. In other respects it is much like that species, the leaves being of similar shape and arrangement, and the flowers of a paler purple; the raceme, however, is only 2 inches or so long'.

E. scoparia—see under Tree Heaths, p. 136.
E. stricta—see under Tree Heaths, p. 136.

ERICA TETRALIX

(*Greek* tetra, *four*, *and* helix, *a spiral*, *from the arrangement of the leaves*)

As the *ciliaris* heath is more at home in the south and hardier there than elsewhere, so *E. Tetralix*, the Cross-leaved Heath, is a natural plant of the north country. The former grows quite well on drier grounds than *Tetralix*, which enjoys the cool moist places of the hills, where it is seen at its best. But the plant is by no means confined to the peat areas as it flourishes in many parts of the British Isles. It has produced varieties of superb merit, for example, *Praegeri*, Con. Underwood and *Mackaiana plena*.

The leaves, about $\frac{1}{8}$ inch long, with glandular hairs along the edges, are set in crosswise whorls of four, which give the plant its name. Their green shade, with white underneath, is prominent in the native type and variable in tones of silvery-grey among the varieties. These mixed shades in the foliage form a number of charming contrasts and, quite apart from the flowers, are an attractive feature of the heather garden. The cylindrical corolla, $\frac{1}{4}$ inch long, is very much contracted at the mouth, the flowers in groups of four and upwards are a waxy, rosy pink, drooping a little at the terminals. Average height is nine inches, and the period of blooming covers a long season, from June to October. Even as late as November the faded corollas are picturesque.

Ciliaris and *Tetralix* are so much alike that there appears to be hardly any difference between the two and it is easy to become confused. In both leaves and flowers the arrangement shows distinct variations. The leaves of *Tetralix* are in fours, those of *ciliaris* in threes; the flowers of the former are very close to the stem, in nodding terminal umbels, but the latter appear along an extended axis where the leaves are smaller than those of the main stems.

Certain plants of the garden, outside the range of the heaths and heathers, require watching closely, otherwise losses are liable to occur owing to fly attack or drought or some other worry. But one may sleep forty days and forty nights and turn over again knowing full well that no harm ever came to our old friend *Tetralix*. I have never lost a single plant and I grow nearly all the varieties—nor have I seen one injured in any way.

VARIETIES OF ERICA TETRALIX

alba   June-August   9 *inches*

I came across a number of excellent specimens of this native plant
below the summit of Snaefell in the Isle of Man, on the moor close
to where the road to Sulby takes a deep bend. It is in moorland
country that I have found good plants of the pure white *Tetralix*.
Heather nurseries list it at a reasonable price.

alba mollis   June-October   9 *inches*

The foliage has a silvery sheen, so striking as to be uncommon
among heaths, and the flowers are a clear white. A distinct plant, as
the leaves are variegated, the green deepening each year on the
older portion in contrast to a much lighter shade on the new growth.
Then during the spring and summer months the silvery tones
become more manifest and as they develop to their full beauty the
effect of the whole is very pleasing. These gradual changes of colour
from one season to another are a feature in the foliage among
heathers.

Strange that *T. alba mollis* is about the only plant in our garden
which fails to grow to normal size, although it is sound enough and
flowers well. I had a bed of plants stunted for years, they would not
increase their stature above a few inches, and I could only assume
there was something wrong with the soil—perhaps there was too
much acid in it and a dressing of lime may have been beneficial.
They have improved since but not to what they should be. I wonder
if readers have a similar experience to report.

It should be noted that the period of blooming is a long one and
as these lines are written early in January the faded blooms are still
on the plants.

Con. Underwood   June-October   9 *inches*

A new variety, which I have only recently planted, and consider
one of the best introductions. The silvery foliage combined with
a crimson bell, probably larger than the other varieties, brings to
the *Tetralix* varieties something of a novel nature.

L. E. Underwood.   June-September   9 *inches*

Another new arrival, a pretty plant, of unusual colour. From the
silver grey leaves there emerges a terracotta bud which opens to
an apricot flower.

Darleyensis   July-August   6 *inches*

I have grown this plant as long as I can remember and it always attracts me. The leaves are a distinct grey-green, the flowers salmon coloured, the habit free and loose in curling stems and lovely nodding bells. It has a charm all its own.

Mackaiana   July-August   6 *inches*

Although usually classified as *Tetralix* opinion is divided and according to Dr Robert Lloyd Praeger it is undoubtedly entitled to rank as a distinct species, as proved by a study of the leaf-anatomy by Miss Margaret Smith (*The Botanist in Ireland*, pages 130-2). Dr Praeger states further that it was found at Craiggamore (Ireland) by William M'Alla prior to 1835. It is a delightful little plant with bright pink bells, in flower during summer months. A double form, *Mackaiana plena*, is equally good, if not better, the flowers being large and rose-pink.

Lawsoniana   July-September   6 *inches*

Another Irish variety, of excellent merit, the flowers being a more subdued and paler pink, and there is a greyish shade in the leaves.

Mary Grace   June-October   6 *inches*

I saw this plant for the first time recently and the striking silvery-grey foliage appealed to me at once. It is a very good form of *Tetralix*, producing a succession of bright pink flowers.

Pink Glow   July-August   9 *inches*

Compared with the Irish *Mackaiana* varieties this is rather disappointing. A good plant without the 'glow' for there is not much glow to be seen. The blooms, on the small side, are freely produced and the silvery-grey leaves distinguish it from the others.

Praegeri   July-September   6 *inches*

This is one of the outstanding varieties in the *Tetralix* group. In the summer of 1949 when it was exceptionally dry, I had a bed of about fifty plants which had been moved in the spring, and when in full bloom they were a magnificent show. Previously the plant appeared in single isolated specimens at some distance from each other, but in growing them together the effect was different again. I regard *Praegeri* as the brightest among the pinks, and I venture to add that it produces more flowers and blooms longer than most, throughout the summer and into autumn. The habit is dwarf as the many stems are closely knitted together and the bells far too numerous to count.

rubrum   July-September   6 *inches*

Rarely seen in our gardens, a fine red, and well worth cultivating.

Ruby's Variety   July-October   6 *inches*

Two colours of the flower characterise this attractive plant; for the most part white, it contrives to change to a purplish pink.

Silver Bells   June-October   6 *inches*

The latest variety, at the time of going to press. A silvery shade in the pink bells produces a pleasing soft mauve.

Another is *praecox alba*, with which I am not familiar.

TREE HEATHS

Although it seems unfortunate that the tree heaths are very limited in number—there are about six altogether—what they lack in quantity they amply repay in quality. I have seen them growing naturally on and below Primrose Hill at Sulby in the Isle of Man, amid gorse and bracken and woodland trees, in a setting overlooking a luxuriant glen not far from the sea. In a climate free from the normal hazards of a winter on the mainland with its sudden temperature changes and damaging late frosts, they were as perfect in shape, foliage and flower as one could wish them to be; and I have no hesitation in saying that in such ideal conditions of pure air, sunshine and moisture-laden winds, they appeared to me the most beautiful heaths I have seen.

It is not everyone who is fortunate enough to enjoy the landscape features which have been developed so skilfully at Sulby. Not the least among the hundreds of choice shrubs to be found there—and many uncommon for the north country—are the heaths and heathers, for it is to the credit of the chief gardener that he is a heather fan. The tree heaths are part of his treasures.

The conditions with me on the Pennines are very different, but there is this to be said about these heaths: if the flowers are liable to injury at a critical period of their development, the consoling alternative of beautiful foliage remains to bring pleasure at all times. The tree heaths are hardly surpassed as winter evergreens, and to those who are planning the winter garden let me commend them as an attractive feature when the days are the shortest.

Erica arborea

The tallest, and often considered the finest of all heaths in shape and form, leaf and flower, in stature anything from five to twenty feet according to locality. I have never come across a specimen more than six feet in height, but I understand it grows much taller in Devon and Cornwall, the Scillies and the Isle of Wight. The smooth linear leaves, in whorls of threes, about ¼ inch long, are thickly clustered, each tiny fin resembling a miniature pine which seems quite fragile compared with the strong stems and many branches growing upwards from the base and giving character and solidity to the tree. Some of the offshoots bend irregularly and gracefully away, thus contrasting with the upright habit of what is a noble object. It will be noticed how neat and close in contact to each other are the leaves as they cover the tree in profusion. They are lighter in colour as the flowers appear and darker in greyish-green when the flowering period is well past—this contrast in light and shade of the foliage is a charming feature.

In November appear pinhead buds which expand imperceptibly and droop slightly in terminal clusters; they can be seen very near the ends of the fine stalks of which there are many. As these lines are written (in December) I am holding a small branch, about five inches long, in my hand, and there are over fifty flower buds on it. As this is merely a fraction of the tree it will give some idea of the tremendous number of flowers to bloom. Each flower, although quite small in itself, is globular, almost white—perhaps one would say ashen-white—and exudes a pleasant odour not unlike the fragrance of honey. (I have grown *arborea* in a pot, quite apart from out of doors, and when bringing it into the house in flower the room is delicately scented by its distillation.)

E. arborea alpina

In addition to its much hardier reputation, this is generally accepted as the more satisfactory plant of the two, but one is reluctant to make comparisons between them. *Arborea* must be judged by its grace and elegance as a tree, *a. alpina* by its compactness as a bush, each to its own sphere of distinction. Their lofty pinnacled branches are to the garden what Gothic architecture is to a building. The foliage alone distinguishes one from the other, *arborea* a more sombre green, *alpina* a vivacious green and much lighter in shade.

Allowing for what has been written in appreciation of these most desirable garden subjects, I must confess to a slight disappointment by the absence of bloom for a few years after planting. This is a general experience with the spring tree heaths, which do not show flower until they have attained a fair age. Once they begin to bloom there is no stopping them, and *a. alpina* will be completely covered with blossoms. A shrub of outstanding merit, indispensable to the garden, it has never failed at Kew in hardiness, habit and flower since it was introduced half a century ago.

E. australis

The Spanish Heath, about six feet tall, in flower the most beautiful of all, a warm, rosy-red, brighter and larger in bell than any other. Its richness of colour surpasses anything I have seen in the heather garden, and if only it was as hardy as the *mediterranea* group or even *stricta*, what a treasure it would be. Unfortunate losses during severe winters have made it rather scarce.

Like other tree heaths, the flowers appear on the previous year's growth, and are almost half an inch long, in clusters of up to as many as eight on the terminal shoots. The flowering period is of exceptional duration, from March onwards to nearly June. Foliage, too, is in keeping with the individual brilliance of its blooms, the rather narrow linear leaves, set in whorls of four about ¼ inch long, displaying a smooth shiny green.

A variety, *australis* Mr Robert, producing a white flower, was discovered in southern Spain by the late Lieut. Robert Williams, who was killed in action in the Great War of 1914-18 and who never saw the tree growing in England. It is on record that Williams searched hard and long before he found this remarkable tree in the mountains near Algeciras and the name afterwards given to it by Mr W. J. Bean at Kew is a fitting tribute to a man who loved plants and who made the supreme sacrifice.

This is a tree heath that stands out above all others and is still without a rival.

There is another variety of *australis* named Riverslea; the rosy-red flowers are a deeper shade and larger than the older form.

E. lusitanica (syn. codonodes)

This Portuguese Heath appears in our gardens more than *E. australis* because it is probably hardier, though there is not much to choose between the two on this account. Even after a bad battering in a very hard winter it usually recovers later in the year with new growth coming from the base, while *australis* under similar conditions invariably fails altogether.

Growing from five to ten feet, *E. lusitanica* spills a rich harvest of blossom in March and April, and a little earlier in the year in warm, sheltered corners. It is in every way a first-class heath; the white flowers, slightly fragrant, are more bell-shaped than globular, as they emerge near the ends of the twigs. There is a tinge of pink in the buds and stamens. Another feature is the large plumose branches, the leaves about ¼ inch long being a palish green. A fully developed specimen grown in a suitable situation, as well as in a favourable locality, is just a dense mass of bloom and branches—in this respect, the most prolific of heaths.

E. scoparia

The Besom Heath suffers by comparison, as it falls rather flat, certainly below the standard of the rest. While the leaf axils are crammed with bloom, the small green flowers have no claim to distinction and hardly any to beauty. They appear (in May and June) in clusters of two to five; the long, linear, deep green leaves are set in whorls of threes. This shrub, which grows to a height of ten feet, fails to maintain a well-branched habit, and the older it is the more out of shape it becomes. Its branches have been used for making besoms in France.

There is a variety *E. scoparia pumila* (syn. var. *nana*) of prostrate habit, up to two feet, bearing a similar type of flower, and, like the larger tree, glossy green leaves.

E. stricta (The Corsican Heath)

The name indicates the character of this tree heath, which has an erect habit, a feature that alone distinguishes it from the others. The new foliage in early summer is of a striking light green shade at the tips in direct contrast to the natural and matured tone of the moss-green leaves, which are deeper in shade as the life of the tree advances. These leaves are borne in whorls of four to six together, and when grown as a hedge, for which *E. stricta* is well suited, the massing of the plumose branches has a telling effect, in itself very pleasing and quite independent of the flowers. A still further contrast is the flower's lovely pale rose colour against the more sombre tones of the foliage. The flowers, appearing in terminal umbels, of four to eight blossoms, are cylindrical.

The height of *E. stricta* varies; in some parts of the south and west it reaches eight feet, in the north between four and five feet. Fading blooms of most garden plants have to be removed because they become untidy, and, towards the fall of the year, somewhat bedraggled after heavy rains. Not so this heath, which has two seasons, one when it is in flower, and the other when it is not—an unusual feature for any plant. *E. stricta* begins to flower in July and its long period of bloom runs well into the autumn; even in December it still retains a picturesque reminder of its summer beauty, like a mirror reflecting the sweetness of the past. Then throughout the succeeding months the fading russet-red bells infuse warmth and colour into the winter garden. Not until the spring should the flower heads be removed, if they are still on the tree.

E. Veitchii

Grows up to six feet, and is a hybrid between *arborea* and *lusitanica*, with many of their characteristics. Discovered in this country in R. Veitch & Sons' Exeter nursery, it ought to be as sturdy, and perhaps it may be hardier than its parents, but almost everything depends on the locality where the tree is grown. It must have shelter from cold winds.

The foliage attracts the eye, especially early in the year, the flowers are white and very fragrant. *Veitchii* in our garden came from Darley Dale, and usually I have a quiet word of prayer that it will stay the course from January to April. It is not as compact as *arborea alpina*, a bush of which stands only a few feet away from it in the background. If the positions were reversed (they should not be) the Veitchii of looser shape and fewer branches would be partly hidden by the more vigorous *a. alpina*.

According to Mr Bean, *Veitchii* appears to be of accidental origin, but there is no doubt as to its parentage. In an interesting note he says: 'It is intermediate in many respects between them. In the colour of its foliage it resembles *E. lusitanica*, but the habit is rather that of *E. arborea*. The flowers are intermediate in shape, and white. They show their hybrid origin in the shape and colour of the stigma, the flattened shape being that of *E. lusitanica*; stamens pink. A further indication of hybridity is in the hairs on the young shoots, which are partly branched like those of *E. arborea*, and partly simple like those of *E. lusitanica*.'

ERICA UMBELLATA

(Latin umbella, *a parasol, from the flower formation)*

If it were not so tender this heath would occupy a permanent place in every heather garden, for it is a very beautiful plant, which blooms just when it is needed, late in the spring, helping to bridge the gap between the spring and summer flowers. The winter varieties have faded and the spring ones are about over as *umbellata* steps in to maintain the flowering sequence.

Only hardy in a mild winter, more than fifteen degrees of frost it will not stand without injury and in anything approaching the hazards of 1947 it is beyond survival. Even in a frame mine was killed in 1941. Not only keen frost but a cold March wind is an enemy to this plant which comes from south-west Europe. I do not frankly advise growing it out of doors north of Nottingham, but in sheltered parts of Wales, Surrey and Sussex, in Devon and Cornwall, and, in warm locations facing south, *umbellata* should come through the average winter immune from serious damage.

The bright rose, globular flowers turn into a rich red before fading; they are freely produced from the umbels, and the leaf formation in the foliage is very fine.

A lime lover, flowers in April and May; height about a foot. R.H.S. Award of Merit.

ERICA VAGANS

(Latin vagans, *wandering)*

A fully developed *vagans* heath is more of a bush than a plant, in height from two to three feet and four to six feet wide. It is exceptionally robust and hardy, perfectly symmetrical in habit, of first-class flowering rank, and an ideal subject for most soils in which it successfully and quickly becomes established. Few other plants are as easy to grow as *vagans* and, with well over a thousand in the garden, I can honestly say that not one has ever given me an anxious moment. The smooth, glossy green leaves are retained the whole year round, making a bright and useful contribution to the winter garden.

Up in the north *vagans* is assured of a permanent place, and its

Part of the heather garden at the R.H.S. Gardens at Wisley.

Erica stricta the Corsican Heath, growing luxuriously in the gardens of Tresco Abbey in the Scillies.

Left: The blush-pink azalea Hinomayo is one of many which may be used to provide colour in parts of the heath garden which are not in flower at the same time.

Below: The intriguing crimped buds and beautiful white pink-marked blooms of *Kalmia latifolia.*

Right: The white flowers of *Leucothoë Catesbaei* appear in May.

Below: The lavish panicles of white flowers of *Pieris Forrestii.*

A barn in Surrey thatched with locally cut heather.

Beehives brought up to the moors when the heather is in flower, to obtain the rich, red heather honey.

healthy constitution remains unbroken. It thrives in a humid atmosphere where the rainfall is fairly heavy, and is seen at its best in the luscious dew after dawn on the fringe of a moor. It revels in loamy soil, prefers loam to peat, and will do better in a poor soil than a rich one.

Vagans has stood the test of zero winters and treacherous winds, its one and only minor injury being an occasional split stem caused by severe frost and heavy weight of ice on the plant. Going to the other extreme of our climate, it resists drought remarkably well, and in the hot dry summer of 1949 those plants cut from the layers and others moved in the spring settled down without showing signs of distress, and it was not until early June, just before the rain came, that they were watered. In the last few rows I found it necessary to heap saturated granulated peat round the roots in planting.

That *vagans* will give satisfaction in surburban and near-to-town gardens there is no disputing. I have seen it in parks surrounded by a network of residential property and industrial works, where aubrieta has been known to fail owing to chemicals in the atmosphere. A *vagans* Lyonnesse plant was in good health and in full flower within two miles of Trafford Park, Manchester.

Viewed from every angle the 'wandering' heath, as *vagans* is called, is a plant of all-round sterling character in flower, foliage, and habit. It adapts itself comfortably and readily without fuss or favour to many situations in diversified parts of the British Isles, even very near to where commerce has a more important place than horticulture, no less freely than in its native ground of Cornwall. And in our own little garden plots we do not make anything like enough of it, we do not cultivate it as we should do. I would like to see hundreds more.

The principal feature in *vagans* is the long cylindrical raceme, from four to eight inches, along which the flowers open at intervals, those below appearing first and fading well before the last at the end are in bloom. These recurring blossoms (which bulge in the centre) build up the floral beauty of the plant, and those which have faded lose none of their charm. The stems are stiff, sturdy and upright, the linear leaves in whorls of four or five—and sometimes more—are about half an inch long, narrow, smooth and dark green. The native flower is a purplish pink and in the varieties we find a number of pleasing colours.

VARIETIES OF ERICA VAGANS

alba   August-September   2 *feet*

The first white to appear, now partly eclipsed by Lyonesse, a better
and larger flower. Despite this, I still think the former is a good
plant, as it always produces plenty of bloom and the foliage is a
lively green.

carnea   August-September   18 *inches*

Light pink flowers, a compact form.

Cream   August-October   2 *feet*

James Smith & Son, of Darley Dale, Derbyshire, introduced this
as a seedling and an improved form of *alba*—and it certainly is.
I have grown the plant for a long time and found it entirely satisfactory. The flowers are a rich creamy shade, while those of *alba*
are a dull white by comparison.

grandiflora   August-September   3 *feet*

The name is well chosen: the spikes are long and packed with vivid
pink blooms, which deepen to red before the flower fades. One of
the best of the group as a quick-growing plant; so strong is its
growth that it should be kept within bounds and not allowed to
become straggly and untidy as we sometimes see it. Cut back hard,
remove all faded blooms each spring.

Kevernensis alba   August-October   1 *foot*

A choice white, quite different from Lyonesse; a compact bushy
dwarf. I find it useful for substantially increasing stock by layering,
the large number of small and young green leaves rooting readily.
The flowers, on the small side, are numerous.

Lyonesse   August-October   18 *inches*

Among all whites under cultivation in the heather world this plant
from Cornwall is in a class apart and has received an Award of
Merit from the R.H.S. The pale brown anthers are in relief to the
smooth, ivory-white flowers which are so numerous as to cover the
plant to overloading capacity. Rich glossy green leaves contribute
much to its beauty. A succession of bloom from August to the end of
September, and when it fades off in October it is still an attractive plant.

Miss Waterer   August-September   18 *inches*

This little-known plant was introduced to me some years ago by the Slieve Donard Nursery in Northern Ireland; it does not appear to be listed elsewhere. A delicate shell-pink and a lighter foliage than other varieties, it was found by Miss Waterer in Cornwall, and has all the virtues of its native companions. I hope that it will be more widely grown. It is hardy, reliable and neat in habit, and I have increased the stock considerably.

Mrs D. F. Maxwell   August-October   18 *inches*

No heather bed is complete without this beautiful heath, which is a great favourite. It at once attracts the eye by its warm cherry pink blossoms, contrasting so distinctly with the dark green foliage. When the bud opens there is depth of tone in the cerise flower and as the bloom matures a rich glowing colour brings out the full beauty of the plant. The spikes are long and bountiful—and for two months of the year it enjoys a high place as a plant of outstanding garden merit, often seen where few other heaths are grown. It well deserves the R.H.S. Award of Merit.

nana   August-September   6 *inches*

A neat dwarf, creamy-white flowers, and chocolate-coloured anthers. Good subject for the rockery.

pallida   August-September   18 *inches*

Pale-pink flowers, a pleasing break from some of the other varieties. Produces many blooms.

Pyrenees Pink   August-September   18 *inches*

I have not grown this compact plant long enough to describe its merits, but I understand the tone of pink seems brighter and perhaps a little deeper than any other vagans. It does not approach Mrs D. F. Maxwell in depth of colour, but has a superior habit to that fine variety.

rosea   August-September   18 *inches*

This new variety, some plants of which reached me only the other day, is a vigorous, growing form of the vagans heath, and very sturdy in habit. The flowers are a warm rose colour.

rubra   August-October   18 *inches*

As the name implies the flowers are red—a rich ruby-red, but in my collection there is a trace of purple in some plants. Confusion has occurred among growers between this plant and *grandiflora*, but the latter is far more vigorous and easily distinguished. The summer of 1949 was so dry that not one here was in flower until mid-September, which was very late. They were still blooming on the 5th of November!

St. Keverne (*kevernensis*) August-September   18 *inches*
Although *vagans* has no more than a round dozen varieties, three have qualified for recognition by the R.H.S. which gave an Award of Merit to St. Keverne in 1927. The flowers, borne in profusion, are a clear, bright pink, and the plant retains its compact habit if trimmed annually.

Erica Veitchii—see under Tree Heaths, p. 137.

HYBRIDS

Darleyensis	January-April	18 *inches*
Dawn	June-October	9 *inches*
F. White	June-October	9 *inches*
George Rendall	January-April	1 *foot*
Gwavas	June-October	1 *foot*
Gwen	June-October	6 *inches*
H. Maxwell	June-October	1 *foot*
Stuartii	June-September	9 *inches*
Watsonii	July-October	9 *inches*
Winifred Whiteley	June-July	1 *foot*
Williamsiana	July-September	8 *inches*
W. G. Notley	June-August	1 *foot*

Up to fairly recently a hybrid was distributed under the name of *mediterranea darleyensis*, but the R.H.S. have reclassified it as *Erica darleyensis*. A cross between *mediterranea* and *carnea*, which it resembles in foliage, its much larger form brought it within the medium height of the *mediterranea* group.

As a strong, sturdy, quick grower it has scarcely a rival, unless it be *carnea* Springwood; this Derbyshire seedling was found forty to fifty years ago, 1100 feet above sea level, in one of the most exposed nurseries in the British Isles. A good harvest of light rose-purple flowers appears late in the year in sheltered and warm corners of the country, early in the year in colder regions, and the plant continues to bloom for over two months.

Certain forms of my *carnea* heaths with strong upright stems are so precocious in growth that they reach the height of the hybrid *darleyensis*, 18 inches. One of them, which undoubtedly came from *carnea* stock, was cut back to six inches, then pulled to pieces by division of the roots in early May. Many young plants were made from that division and so rapid was their development that they put on over an inch of growth within twelve months and flowered freely in the January following the division of the previous May.

Although there must be some hybrid mixture among the carneas to produce plants as tall as *darleyensis*, I am inclined to believe that growth is very much increased and stimulated in an open, sunny situation and at a high altitude in pure moorland air. For robustness, for quality of both foliage and flower, and for increasing stock by propagating, the carneas which are grown here are far and away better than all other heathers, and it is not surprising that strong hybrids appear from time to time. I will go further and say that the carneas, which eventually are anything from eighteen to twenty inches high, excel *darleyensis*; they are brighter and denser in foliage and produce more flowers.

Long after the Derbyshire seedling had been discovered came the improved hybrid, George Rendall, the flowers of which are a deeper purple than the older plant and the foliage is of a glaucous tint. It is, in addition, more compact, and after the blooms have faded the golden tips of the new growth as well as the fresh lively green of the remaining foliage bring George Rendall into the picture of spring's best plants. It is a fine subject for the background of a rockery.

SUMMER-FLOWERING HYBRIDS

Williamsiana, H. Maxwell, Dawn and Gwen are choice hybrid selections, producing masses of pink flowers over as long a period as June to October. The parentage is *ciliaris* × *Tetralix*, excepting *Williamsiana*, which is a cross between the *vagans*, Cornish heath, and *Tetralix*.

The tips are a bright gold in the spring, brighter than George Rendall, looking more like flowers than a conspicuous part of the foliage. No more than a foot high, they are beautiful subjects for any part of the garden, especially among rock plants.

I regard H. Maxwell as one of the best; it never seems to be out of bloom throughout the summer, and for a plant to be in flower for four consecutive months evokes our whole-hearted enthusiasm and admiration. Large bright pink blossoms bring continual patches of colour into the heather garden.

Williamsiana, a natural hybrid found in Cornwall, inherits the floral charm of the parent, *vagans*, but the foliage is unmistakably that of the moorland *Tetralix*. It is a splendid dwarf heath, pleasant to look at at any time of the year, close in habit, the linear leaves set in whorls of four and ⅛ inch long. Flowers appear at the end of the shoot, the corolla is bell-shaped, rose-pink, with brown anthers. The foliage changes with the seasons from a pale to a lighter green, with a yellowish tint in the new growth and gold tips. Leaf colour shading and warm pink bells (not as numerous as in H. Maxwell and Dawn) make the plant most attractive. I have mentioned elsewhere in this book that certain heaths should be grown more than we find them today in the average garden: this is one.

The difference between the *ciliaris* heath and *Tetralix*, as explained on page 130, is clearly brought out in the hybrid *Dawn*. It will be observed that the stalk follows the habit of *Tetralix* in being elongated, with the flower at the terminal, and the many flowers of a deep rose look well elevated above the foliage which is distinctly *ciliaris*. A very fine hybrid in bloom all through the summer months and early autumn.

Gwen is much smaller than Dawn, a neat dwarf, with a copper shade in the foliage, and bearing plenty of pale pink flowers. Some of these hybrids have Cornish origin; *Watsonii* is no exception as it was found near Truro by Mr H. C. Watson. The large rosy-crimson bells, although of *ciliaris* strain, appear in a flatter raceme than the one which characterises the Dorset heath. It will be seen that the terminal umbels resemble the *Tetralix* plant, and the raceme is not extended to any degree. The narrow leaves follow the arrangement of *Tetralix* in whorls of four.

Quite out of the ordinary is the hybrid W. G. Notley, from Dorset, of which the foliage is that of *cinerea* and the flowers of *Calluna vulgaris*. Rarely does an alliance take place in which Heath and Heather become one and, in this instance, the marriage is highly successful. So deep a pink and so small a flower as we find in W. G. Notley are alike exceptional among heathers, and the bronze-green leaves are clearly of the *cinerea* type. This remarkable cross-strained heath has stood up well in our northern climate and I have no hesitation in saying that it is hardy and reliable.

Dr Robert Lloyd Praeger, in *The Botanist in Ireland*, has some interesting notes on the hybrid *Stuartii*, which he diagnoses as *E. Mackaii* × *mediterranea*. Only one clump was found, at Craiggamore, by Charles Stuart, of Edinburgh, in 1920, growing with *E. Mackaii*, and *E. mediterranea* has its nearest station on Urrisbeg, three miles to the south. The leaves are very fine and the small pink flowers pinched at the tip. It is hard to explain the curiously contracted shape of the flowers. The plant has always done well with me.

Of the remaining hybrids, F. White follows the habit of Dawn, the white flowers having a tint of pink; Gwavas produces a striking yellow colour at the shoot end in the spring foliage and bright pink blooms later; Winifred Whiteley is similar to W. G. Notley.

Menziesia—see *Daboëcia*, p. 96.

CHAPTER IX

SHRUBS AND TREES

The fruit-like perfume of the golden furze
Coleridge

IT would hardly be doing justice to much wider spheres of horticulture if some of their best treasures were excluded from the heather garden; and one may discover, after a little investigation, how many harmonise with a colony of heaths. They make a useful contribution to individual schemes; they help to break up uniformity; they provide a sense of proportion in relation to the contour of the ground, giving effect to heights and furnishing a suitable background; they enhance the charm of the heath garden as a whole.

There follows a list of trees and shrubs most of which are closely allied to the heaths and heathers. Beyond these, there is, of course, a very wide range of non-ericaceous shrubs and trees, from which a selection may also be made, depending on the size and nature of the site; to describe these in detail is beyond the scope of this book, but the names of some are listed at the end of this chapter.

If the soil is peaty or of a texture that retains liberal moisture one could not do better than introduce the andromedas, kalmias, dwarf rhododendrons and other shrubs of this kind such as are described below.

ANDROMEDA
(*see also* Chamaedaphne, Leucothoë, Pieris, Zenobia, *now classified under separate genera*)

polifolia   May   12-18 *inches*

This dwarf evergreen shrub, known as the wild rosemary, is a native of British and Irish peat bogs. It has long, dark, shining, elliptic-lance-shaped leaves, resembling the rosemary, and pinky-white flowers prettily borne in small drooping clusters near the end of the shoots. In garden cultivation it should be grown in peat. Part shade, but preferably in full sun.

150

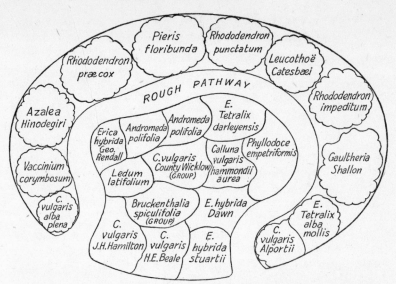

Suggested plans for gardens consisting partly of heathers and partly of shrubs. The one above contains ericaceous shrubs; the other various kinds which will associate equally well with heaths.

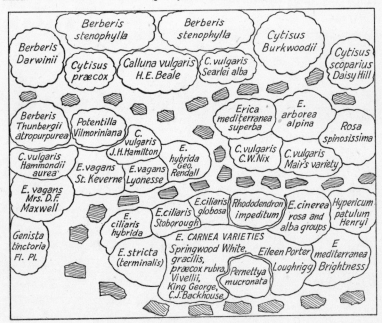

polifolia var. angustifolia May *12-18 inches*
Narrow leaves and clusters of pink bells in the spring.

Azalea—see *Rhododendron.*

ARCTOSTAPHYLOS

Uva-ursi April-May *6-9 inches*
A prostrate creeper, called the Red Bearberry, another native of
Britain, with shining evergreen leaves, red stems and pink flowers in
terminal clusters, followed by red berries. Where the heather garden
borders a shrubbery or woodland this is a useful trailer on the fringe
of the trees, in part shade.

BRUCKENTHALIA

spiculifolia June-July *9 inches*
This plant does very well in our garden; it loves a cool moist soil
and a peaty mixture. Though no more than a foot high, it soon
becomes a tightly packed clump of leaves, which are bright and
finely pointed and evergreen. Pretty rose-pink flowers appear at the
tips of the leaf growth, and although the flowering season is a fairly
short one, it is an exquisite plant when in bloom. Divisions may
be taken from the roots, which are easily divided. I regard it as one
of the best of allied subjects for the heather garden.

Bryanthus—see *Phyllodoce*

Cassandra—see *Chamaedaphne.*

CASSINIA

fulvida July-August *3-4 feet*
A New Zealand shrub, aptly described as the 'Golden Heath'
because of its slender habit and rather narrow deep green leaves
with a golden-yellow colour underneath. Produces tiny daisy-white
flowers profusely, but these are insignificant compared with the
cheerful colour of the foliage, the slight drooping of the branch ends
and the general neatness of the shrub.

CASSIOPE

tetragona May-June *9 inches*
The Lapland Heath, a small upright shrub, each twig coming from
the base, as the very bright leaves overlap so tightly as to suggest
they have been wound by some deliberate invisible hand. They

have the appearance of whipcord. When the plant is in the mood to flower (which is not often, as it is shy in this respect) an exquisite, delicately fragrant white bell modestly decorates the branches like buttonholes. It can only be successfully grown to produce bloom when the plant is in peat—and the stronger the peat the better. I have seen it in perfect flower in feet-deep bog peat, which I have used for this Lapland plant.

CHAMAEDAPHNE

(*syn.* Andromeda *and* Cassandra)

calyculata and
calyculata nana　　　　May-June　　　　1-3 *feet*
Elliptic-oblong, leathery green leaves, and racemes of small, pure white flowers resembling lily of the valley. Although the branches are few, the shrub provides plenty of leaves and flowers. The variety *nana* is well suited for growing among heathers.

ENKIANTHUS

campanulatus　　　　May-June　　　　4-6 *feet*
A Japanese shrub, with sharply toothed leaves, and drooping clusters of creamy-yellow, fringed, flowers.

cernuus　　　　　　　　　　　　　　3-5 *feet*
This variety, although deciduous, has two distinct features—the dullish green leaves turn to a rich crimson in the autumn and the clusters of bell-shaped, creamy-white blossoms adorn the shrub in early summer. It is in every way a good subject among heathers.

GAULTHERIA

procumbens　　　　July-August　　　　6 *inches*
This best-known plant of the species enjoys creeping over much ground, by which its roots are formed. The lustrous green leaves, which give off a strong odour, become reddish late in the year. Pinky-white flowers appear in the summer like lilies of the valley, followed by scarlet berries which the partridge relishes—hence another name given to the shrub—'partridge berry'.

Shallon　　　　May-June　　　　2-4 *feet*
More of a bush than a shrub owing to its dense growth and should

only be planted in the heather garden of spacious dimensions because it increases by underground suckers. Though not particularly rampant, it should not be included in the main colony of heathers, as it might become troublesome by reappearing where it is not wanted, but in partial shade on the *outer* side of a group of trees it is safe enough. I have found that if it gets too much among shrubs neither the flowers nor the fruit are seen at all, in fact one has sometimes to move by hand some of the foliage in order to see the half-hidden, drooping, egg-shaped, pink-white flowers. It is surprising how much bloom is exposed to the light in this way. The juicy, dark purple fruits are edible, and the leaves in the winter, particularly the underside, are red. One should remember that the growth is strong enough to become a thicket.

GAULTHETTYA

wisleyensis   May-June   2 *feet*
Known as 'Wisley Pearl', a chance hybrid between Gaultheria and Pernettya discovered in the Royal Horticultural Society's Gardens at Wisley. It produces clear white lily-of-the-valley flowers and lovely purple berries. It is the Gaulnettya of catalogues.

KALMIA

angustifolia   May-June   2-4 *feet*
A species known as the Canadian Sheep Laurel, with bright evergreen leaves and a rosy-red, saucer-shaped corolla. Varieties include *rubra*, dark red blooms, *pumila* (syn. *nana*), dwarf and crimson, and *rosea*, a pink rose shade.

latifolia   June   10-15 *feet*
One of the loveliest of North American shrubs, called the Calico Bush, and a distinct feature of garden cultivation in Britain. It has smooth, brilliantly glossy oval leaves and large trusses of saucer-shaped blossoms in shades of white, soft pink and deep rose at the ends of the shoots of the previous year's growth.

glauca (or **polifolia**)   April-May   1-2 *feet*
Another American variety, low-growing, producing beautiful rose to pale purple flowers in a terminal cluster, and narrow dark green leaves, white underneath.

It should be clearly noted that the kalmias are peat lovers and on no account should their roots come into contact with lime. They are admirably suited for the heather garden and benefit by added leaf-mould and loam. If enriched in this way and kept moist, they flourish naturally and produce abundant blooms. Half-shaded places and dampish ground suit them well.

LEDUM

groenlandicum (*latifolium*) April-June *2 feet*
The Labrador Tea shrub, of North America, evergreen, narrow, heart-shaped leaves, curled at the edges, and rusty brown underneath. Small white flowers are in clusters at the end of the shoots.

Two other species, *L. glandulosum* (2-3 feet) and *L. palustre* (1-3 feet), both white, as well as *L. groenlandicum* are good subjects for the heather garden, provided there is ample moisture and, if possible, a deep bed of old peat.

LEIOPHYLLUM

buxifolium May-June *9-12 inches*
This is sometimes listed (incorrectly) as *Ledum Lyonii* and is known as the Sand Myrtle, an evergreen from the mountains of Virginia. I have grown it long enough to regard it as perfectly hardy in *very exposed* situations. It is certainly a very pretty plant and has the unusual habit of completely changing its flower colour. As the bud breaks dainty rose-pink blossoms appear in clusters, but when fully open the pink colour has somehow become absorbed and instead is a bunch of white stars—a sort of fluffy finish to the bloom. It almost looks as though some fairy wand had changed the process by magic. The shrub is densely covered with small oval glossy green leaves. I would always choose this most picturesque dwarf shrub for company with the heathers; it is neat, bushy, and original in colour sequence of flower.

LEUCOTHOË

Catesbaei (*Andromeda Catesbaei*) May *3-6 feet*
A very beautiful shrub, with axillary racemes of pure white pitcher-shaped flowers, not unlike the lily of the valley, and arching branches of glossy leaves.

Rollisonii   May   *2-4 feet*
Similar to the above but narrower leaves.

Davisiae   June   *1-3 feet*
The foliage is a dark, shiny green; white flowers.

PERNETTYA

When I first planted Pernettya a long time ago one important matter was overlooked—the mixing of the sexes. The oversight was responsible for the loss of berries. It is well to remember when ordering plants from a nursery that two males should always accompany one female.

The pernettya is a native of the Straits of Magellan, and named after Dom Pernetty, traveller and author; although of South American origin it is remarkably hardy, as well as being robust. It is called the Prickly Heath because the shiny green leaves have prickly tips, hence the appropriate name *P. mucronata*, from the Latin *mucro*—a sharp point.

mucronata   May-June   *2-3 feet*
A sturdy, wiry, upright shrub, with ovate leaves, sharply pointed; in the summer appear small white flowers, succeeded by innumerable clusters of magnificent berries, in varying shades of pink, red, crimson, lilac, purple and violet; some are nearly black in colour and some quite large, up to half an inch. This kaleidoscopic display of fruits enriches the autumn scene and most of the berries remain on the shrub throughout the winter. Berries of nearly all other trees have been devoured by the birds long before March comes round, but those of the pernettyas are not very palatable. Only the blackbird nibbles occasionally in a very hard winter, and on high ground where the atmosphere is keen he nibbles at almost anything.

tasmanica   April-May   *3 inches*
As the name implies, a Tasmanian shrub, of dwarf, prostrate habit, and an unusual species of pernettya. It has very tiny stems, pointed green leaves, white, bell-shaped flowers, and large bright red berries which seem rather out of proportion to the size of the shrub.

While the pernettyas, and their hybrids, including those introduced by Mr Davis, of Hillsborough, grow well in most gardens and are adaptable to all kinds of soil from clay to sand, and from lime to deep loam, they thrive best in moist peat, which improves the standard of the berries in both size and colour. After planting they can be left undisturbed and without pruning for some years. I increase the stock by the simple method of layering the lower side branches, the bent portion from which new root is made being placed in the soil and held down firmly by a stone, the remaining part of the branch growing upward in the ordinary way. These offshoots are cut with a knife when sufficient fresh growth is established.

The pernettyas are ideal subjects for the heather garden.

PHYLLODOCE

empetriformis   April-May   6 *inches*

For some three weeks this comparatively small shrub is a feature of the heather garden, to which it naturally belongs as it so much resembles the heath family. The flowers, much larger than the average heather plant, are handsome, pitcher-shaped, rosy-pink bells, appearing in clusters at the leaf axils near the ends of the stems. Even when not in bloom, the evergreen charm of the very bright glossy green leaves is maintained, so no matter what season of the year it may be, the shrub is a pleasant object in the garden. My plants, of which I have a considerable number, are always cultivated in peat mixed with fibrous loam. Its hardiness is so reliable that the worst winters have never injured the shrub. *P. empetriformis*, sometimes listed as *Bryanthus empetriformis*, is a native of Western North America, and it will give you excellent service for many years, provided it is thrice blessed with an open situation, plenty of sunlight and continual moisture at the roots.

PHYLLOTHAMNUS

erectus   April-May   12-18 *inches*

To spell these names on a typewriter may be easier than to crack one's jaw in pronouncing *Rhodothamnus Chamaecistus* and *Phyllodoce caerulea*, which are said to be the parents of the hybrid *Phyllothamnus erectus!* An ericaceous plant which loves a cool moist spot where no lime is present, but peat or leaf-mould mixed with loam, it has an upright habit, bright green, linear leaves, and clusters of cheerful rose-pink bells at the tip of the stalk. It is the same plant as *Bryanthus erectus*.

PIERIS

floribunda (*Andromeda floribunda*) March-April 3-6 *feet*
Loves a cool, damp soil, in peat and deep leaf-mould; should be
given shelter to protect the early buds from damage by cold winds.
The dark, rich green, leathery leaves, oval and pointed, the pure
white bell-shaped lily-of-the-valley flowers in abundant clusters
borne loftily on stiff, erect spikes at the end of the branches, all
contribute their beauty to this ornamental North American shrub.

Forrestii March-April 5-8 *feet*
A very beautiful species of recent introduction, the particular merit
of which is the pale red tints of the young foliage in spring. It has
larger flowers than the other species.

japonica (*Andromeda japonica*) March-April 5-8 *feet*
Considered even more beautiful than *P. floribunda*, this variety is
not as hardy, and comes from Japan. It produces long spikes—four
to five inches—of pitcher-shaped, wax-white bells, which droop in
pendulous fashion, partially screening the lustrous dark-green
foliage, the new growth of which is beautifully coloured in the
spring. The leaves are particularly striking, pointed, as in *P. floribunda*, and elliptical and serrated. This shrub is suitable for part
shade where it will thrive quite well.

RHODODENDRONS

Dwarf rhododendrons are ideal subjects interspaced with heathers,
as they are closely allied. They thrive in peaty soil, and most of them
do quite well in loam, leaf-mould, liberal dressings from a well-
rotted compost heap (free from lime), and autumn leaves, dug in.
The essential ingredient for flourishing rhododendrons is rich
humus.

Early-flowering varieties are liable to be injured by sharp frosts
which turn the leaves brown in February, and a friend of mine
throws a sheet over *R. praecox* when there is a clear blue evening
sky—a sure indication of a frosty dawn.

As the choice of shrubs is a wide one, only a short selection of
varieties is given, sufficient for the reader's guidance. It should be
remembered that the rhododendron becomes an important part of

Heathers are not easy to arrange as cut flowers, but patience will produce attractive results.

A mass of *Calluna vulgaris* H. E. Beale, in an attractive setting.

a heather garden in which the shrubs are comparatively few and carefully chosen. The following are recommended for planting with heaths.

R. ferrugineum (Central Europe)   May-June   2 *feet*
The familiar Alpine Rose, with innumerable green leaves marked with a rusty brown, and countless numbers of small, rosy-crimson flowers at the terminals of the shoots.

R. glaucum (Sikkim)   April-May   2-4 *feet*
Aromatic, oval leaves, glaucous underneath and nodding, bell-shaped rose-coloured blooms.

R. hirsutum (Switzerland)   May-June   2-3 *feet*
Similar to *R. ferrugineum*, hairy at the leaf edge and underneath; dark-green foliage and small rosy crimson flowers.

R. impeditum (Yunnan)   April-May   12-18 *inches*
A delightful dwarf, rounded bush, neat and compact, in every way suitable for the heather garden. The blooms are a striking shade of light purple which gives the shrub a glowing rosy hue when in full flower. Leaves are fringed with hairs. I would not care to be without it.

R. laetevirens (*Wilsonii*) (Garden hybrid) May-June 18 *inches*
Rose-purple flowers.

R. minus (*punctatum*) (America)   May   4 *feet*
Another choice variety which is admirably suited for growing with ericas. Its bright green foliage and rose-purple flowers blend naturally among the heaths, and as it is taller than most of those described it should be planted at the back where it can be seen to advantage.

R. myrtifolium (Garden hybrid)   June   2 *feet*
Rose-pink blossoms borne in profusion and leaves like the myrtle, bronze-green.

R. praecox (Garden hybrid)   February-March   3 *feet*
This hybrid between *R. ciliatum* and *R. dauricum*, the first to flower, is indispensable. A beautiful form, its red buds and violet-rose flowers are freely displayed in early spring. Looks well as a background to *Erica carnea* Springwood White. It should be given protection as previously advised.

R. racemosum (W. China)   April-May   *1-3 feet*
Bears clusters of pink blossoms from the leaf axils at the ends of the shoots; oval, shiny leaves.

R. tephropeplum (Tibet)   May   *3 feet*
Of bushy growth, long narrow leaves, grey underneath, with trusses of rose-coloured flowers.

R. viscosum (*Azalea viscosa*) (N. America)   June   *4 feet*
A deciduous form, producing beautiful white and pink flowers which are sweetly scented. One of the best for early summer bloom when the heaths are rather subdued in flower. It is known as the American Swamp Pink or Swamp Honeysuckle as the calyx is glandular and sticky.

R. Williamsianum (W. China)   April-May   *12-18 inches*
Shell-pink campanulate flowers in terminal custers.

AZALEAS

A keen gardener once showed me a fine collection of azaleas in full bloom and said he proposed planting heathers between the shrubs. I could not agree to his suggestion as far as the early-flowering heaths were concerned, because the azaleas were so vivid that the colour of the heaths would lose much of its effect. My friend had already covered some of his ground in planting a number of *Erica vagans* Mrs D. F. Maxwell; I could see no objection to this, for the Cornish heaths would be in flower long after the azaleas.

While I am of the opinion that *Azalea mollis* is too showy and much too colourful in the heather garden, and, as far as I am concerned, they are excluded entirely, I would not hesitate to introduce some of the dwarf evergreen varieties, provided the selection was made judiciously. Here are a few which are suggested to help the planter in selecting the appropriate varieties for his heather plot:

A. amoena   Dwarf, magenta-rose flowers, borne in profusion.

A. amoena coccinea A beautiful small shrub, with deep rich crimson blooms.

A. amoena Hexe   Another fine crimson—hose-in-hose flowers.

A. Hinodegiri	Brilliant red single flowers.
A. Hinomayo	Bluish pink.
A. Kirin	The Coral Bell Azalea, double flowers, bright pink.
A. Kaempferi	Only partly evergreen, bearing orange-red flowers of a striking shade.
A. macrantha	Salmon-pink, late flowering.
A. canadense	This could be included in the Rhododendrons as *R. Rhodora* and it is described also as *Rhodora canadensis*. A deciduous shrub, the flowers of pale lilac appear in the spring on bare branches.

Most of these flower in spring or early summer and are dwarf in height. One or two here and there will blend with the heathers.

VACCINIUM

angustifolium var. laevifolium
(*pensylvanicum*)   April-May   *1-2 feet*
Pale pink flowers in early summer, black edible berries, and serrated leaves furnishing beautiful autumn colour.

corymbosum (Tall Blueberry)   May   *4-6 feet*
An attractive shrub, of bell-shaped pink flowers, which remind one of the lily of the valley. The bright green leaves change to brilliant red in the autumn.

Vitis-idaea (Cowberry)   May-June   *9 inches*
Creeping evergreen, shining leaves, pale pink or white flowers, edible red fruits.

Another species one hesitates to include is *V. glaucoalbum*, 2-3 feet; it is not generally hardy and only suitable for mild localities. The bush is resplendent in blue-white colour on both the fruits and the undersides of the leaves; in direct contrast is the palish pink flower.

ZENOBIA

pulverulenta (speciosa)   June-July   *4 feet*
(*Andromeda pulverulenta*)
This is one of the loveliest of shrubs, which is sometimes listed

under the andromedas, and should always have a place in the heather garden where the area is large enough. Even in smaller plots it is well worth growing. The lily-of-the-valley flowers which are so conspicuous a part of the whole family are seen to the fullness of their beauty in the zenobias. An additional feature which enhances the merit of the shrub is the glaucous bloom on the leaves.

NON-ERICACEOUS TREES AND SHRUBS

Below is a list of some of the trees and shrubs which will associate well with heathers.

Acer palmatum var. *atropurpureum, p.* var. *dissectum.*
Berberis aggregata var. *Prattii, Darwinii, D.* var. *prostrata, stenophylla, Thunbergii* var. *atropurpurea.*
Cytisus albus, Ardoinii, Burkwoodii, kewensis, nigricans, praecox, scoparius var. *prostratus, s.* var. *sulphureus.*
Fabiana imbricata.
Genista cinerea, pilosa, sagittalis, tinctoria fl. pl.
Hypericum patulum var. *Henryi,* Rowallane hybrid, *reptans.*
Lavandula officinalis var. *compacta.*
Polygala Chamaebuxus.
Potentilla fruticosa var. *Vilmoriniana.*
Rosa nitida, pendulina (alpina), spinosissima.
Spartium junceum.
Ulex Gallii.

CHAPTER X

THE USES OF HEATHER

As heather has long found a place in the practical heads of the people it has come to mean something more than a plant of the heath. Sowerby's *English Botany* reminds us that it is not merely as the child of the mountain fastnesses, associated with Scotland in all its legends, and almost as national an emblem as the bagpipe, that the Highlander values this little plant—'to him it is something more than a mere badge of clanship, it furnishes him with much that is valuable in his daily life.'

CUT BLOOMS

In July and August each year sprays of white heather are cut for the florists' market. One large nursery reserves part of its acreage for this side of the business, cultivating only those plants which produce long sprays of beautiful white blooms. I have watched men at this nursery bending their backs while cutting at Hammondii or Mair's variety, two of the best white heathers for this purpose. *Searlei alba* is also cut, and *torulosa* is a plant of very pretty sprigs. It is a tedious, perspiring job which demands much patience and steady work throughout a hot summer's day. After the sprays are cut, they are weighed and tied in bundles of one pound, and it is usual to charge by the pound. Since the war this trade has fluctuated, partly through stocks lost heavily during the war and partly arising out of labour shortage. Few men are prepared to do this sort of work to-day, for a wage which compares unfavourably with the high rates of pay offered by factories. When labour was cheaper more men were available and about £400 passed through a nursery's books from the sale of heather bloom in a brief period of a few weeks.

Most people imagine that the sprays of 'Lucky Scotch White Heather' all come from Scotland; in actual fact, few of them do. Most of the bunches sold over the Border have been cut from plants grown in Derbyshire. I have myself had an insight to this side of the business between Derbyshire and Scotland which has reached considerable proportions during the present century. An old Scotch neighbour of mine tells me with a twinkle in his eye that when he has bought a sprig of white heather in Glasgow he knew full well that it had come from within a few miles of where he lived. But no one in Scotland believed him!

These cut white blooms are sent all over the British Isles, largely to the florists, and a lot passes through the wholesale markets before being sold to the shops. Several tons are disposed of in a couple of months.

They are used in a variety of ways, for table decoration, in hotels, boarding-houses and in the home, for charity appeals, as button-holes, lucky charms at race meetings, hawkers' wares at the street curb (although I think some of these are 'fakes'), wedding bouquets, funeral wreaths, and emblems for calendars and souvenirs.

While there would appear to be a wide field for this industry and plenty of opportunities for developing enterprising markets, one would have to grow a large number of plants to make it worth while and really profitable. And a lot of plants require a fair amount of ground—half an acre, at least, for the cultivation of Hammondii, *alba plena*, Mair's variety, *tomentosa* and *Searlei*.

The chances of better financial returns in spring should not be ruled out as flowers fetch higher prices early in the year. Such species as *carnea* Springwood White, *mediterranea alba* and *m.* W. T. Rackliff, *arborea* and *Veitchii* produce attractive flowers, although it seems to be spoiling tree heaths to cut them in this way.

There is another side of this white heather trade which is asso-ciated with sentiment, or tradition—call it superstition, if you like—that is not so apparent in the spring-flowering heaths as it undoubt-edly is in the Lucky White Heather of summer and autumn. I have offered spring-flowering white heath blooms to friends, who have solemnly wagged their heads and dryly remarked: 'Very beautiful, I agree, but it's not *WHITE HEATHER* … you know what I mean, *that White Heather which comes from Scotland in August!*' It is no use arguing, no use talking further, Highland mythology still haunts their minds and sentiment lies deep in their hearts.

Apart from table decoration, sprays of half-faded heather bells are used for calendars and greeting cards by leading firms as emblems of good luck. Sprays are also used in connection with souvenir articles for customers and are sold by certain charity organisations for the purpose of raising money. Another avenue of trade, more in the nature of a side line, is with professional hawkers sending a postal-order to a nursery for a supply of cut white heather prior to a race meeting.

Cut blooms last a long while, provided they receive a change of water about once a fortnight. If sent away, they are easily packed, occupy little space, and in damp moss remain fresh for an indefinite period. Sprays of *Alportii* and H. E. Beale which we bring into the house in August and September are not discarded until the following February. Even the fading bells are pleasant to look at, as their beauty mellows with the passing of autumn.

BESOMS AND BROOM-MAKING

One of the oldest of rural industries is that of broom-making, cutting heather for brushes and besoms after the sap has risen but before the blossom is formed. This means a fairly early start in the season when the broom-maker begins his work, some time about the end of June, after he has come to terms with the owner of the heather ground. He and his ancestors carried on the trade for many generations, and a writer of half a century ago describes them in this way:

'They were said to be of high-class gipsy descent, brown, sinewy and strong, these Fergusons and Stuarts (the royal spelling of the name is insisted upon), and they revelled in their weeks on the hills. Coming from a distance, they pitch their tents around the heather and begin their pleasant work, aided by sharp blades and plenty of tarred string. The women accompany them, and boil their well-filled pots and kettles outside, hung over the crackling fire. Then during the day the women hawk provisions in the neighbourhood, buying and selling and bearing their heavy burdens easily and lightly.'

This healthy family of gipsy blood is as tough as the heather from which they earn honest coppers.

For brooms heather is cut long, the longer the better, and tied in bundles, varying in weight from 2 stones (28 lb.) upwards. Heather besoms are still made in Dorset, Surrey, Yorkshire, Derbyshire, parts of Wales, and in the Ulverston district. A heather besom is softer and more pliable than birch, and is sometimes used in the steel plate industry for throwing the water on to the steel.

Owing to post-war economic conditions beyond their control, some heather cutters are working solely for themselves rather than engaging labour at a remuneration which, competitive with other trades, would make heather cutting unprofitable. I have mentioned in the chapter on the wild ling the rural industry of contract cutting, where the owner of a moor fixes a certain price according to the amount of ground allocated to the tenant, who cuts heather and supplies it to various markets at prearranged contract rates. The cut branches are used for broom-making, brushes, summer-houses, and packing sanitary fittings against which the heather is more resistant than straw or shavings. At one time a hired cutter was paid three shillings a day, for which he worked fairly long hours and turned out as many as ten bundles, each weighing slightly under 30 lb. Wages have now no fixed scale and vary according to arrangements made in the locality where the work is still carried on.

THATCHING

The heather builder and thatcher comes a little later for his materials. He builds cattle-houses, fowl-houses, pavilions and summer huts—very warm and picturesque they are; he makes garden ornaments, such as bird pedestals and cotes roofed with heather thatch. After forty years a summer hut in my neighbourhood had not been renewed with fresh material. It is strong, durable and watertight.

On receiving an order, the heather thatcher measures the area to be covered, height, circumference, and slope of roof. Then, with a trained eye, he decides how many bundles will be required. Although occasionally a thatcher will cut his own heather on the moor, it is usual for him to buy it from a man who spends most of his time there.

The heather is cut about 14 inches long and bound in bundles of about 3 to 4 inches round, which is usually the right thickness, although this varies according to the work in hand. Stout poles form a framework for the building; these are driven deep into the ground, and are about 7 feet high above ground. Across them stretch smaller poles, 6 inches apart, and to these the bundles are tied, blossom outside and stalks sloping in. The bundles are pressed very close and each row overlaps the lower one, forming a compact mass. The roof tapers to a point, where a piece of wood finishes it, and a weathercock or flag or some similar object is attached, to meet the customer's requirements.

When all this is done the heather branches are clipped to shape with a hedge clipper and cut on top leaving an even surface, or they are shaped to a pattern if required. Cut heather for an old-established firm of makers of rustic work known to the writer comes from Yorkshire in a railway truck; it arrives in bloom and the flowers are trimmed off later.

To the extent that heather thatching is carried out today in dwelling houses, I am indebted to the Thatching Instructor of the Rural Industries Bureau for this up-to-date information:

'Heather thatching is preferred by some people because of the very attractive colour to which it tones, in the course of time.

'There are few thatchers who would recommend its use without the roof first being covered with feather-edge boarding or a thin layer of straw thatch. This is because of the difficulty in making the roof water-tight due to (a) shortness of heather and (b) its woody nature which does not allow it to work together closely and is therefore less compact.

'It has another peculiar characteristic, in that birds will not attack it as there is some smell or taste about it which they do not like.

'The method of thatching in Scotland is to apply a layer of heather and then a layer of bog peat alternately, until the whole area of the roof is covered, the bog peat being all that holds the thatch in position except in exposed districts where a form of string netting is used as a protection against excessive wind.'

According to this authority, heather for thatching of dwelling houses is used less than one per cent compared with all other materials, and it applies otherwise and mainly to summer houses, lich-gates and similar ornamental features already mentioned.

BEES AND HONEY

In moorland country many beehives are transported annually to the heather. The practice of removing bees to fresh pastures is said to come from the Egyptians, who followed the honey-bearing flowers as the home crop failed. North-country beekeepers maintain a keen eye on heather in flower and when, walking through it, pale brown powder sticks to their boots they know it for the honey powder and at once begin preparations. The summer flowers are over, so no more honey will be made from them; but with the heather a new and more valuable harvest begins; the hives are packed up, and transported to the moors for a season.

Heather honey is red in colour and rich in flavour. It has a fragrance that is different from anything else in the larder, and when the top of a jar is removed one gets a sudden and welcome whiff of the moors.

As to the revenues these trades, or at least some of them, yield annually, no precise figures are available; nor is there any official record of the country's returns in the sale of honey. Inquiries made at H.M. Stationery Office confirm this lack of information.

In addition to thatching, beds are made from heather, which is laid in a sloping direction, blossom upwards, roots turned outwards, so that the most comfortable part lies down the centre. With a plaid over it, as one procures in Scotland, it provides a soft, springy resting place, as many will agree who have slept on a heather bed.

Heather branches are used for heating ovens, making scrubbing brushes and baskets, for weaving into fences, for covering underground drains, for packing fittings, pipes and similar material. 'In forming roads across marshy ground, as an intermediate layer between a bottoming of brushwood and a top surface of gravel': so writes Mr H. L. Edlin of another use for heather in his book, *Woodland Crafts in Britain*. He also mentions that *Cuacks* or drinking cups were made in Perthshire, from segments of heather wood, bound together with willow withes. 'Bundles of stiff twigs, called *renges*, were used in the Highlands as pot scrubbers before the introduction of piassava fibre. The roots of heather served as nails or pegs, for such purposes as hanging slates.'

Medicinally, heather contains certain astringent properties, which come from the shoots.

Portions of the plant when crushed and steeped in alum water produce a kind of heath-tan of golden hue, and in the Highlands a housewife dyes her goods a fine yellow with this heather and alum.

In the western Highlands heather is twisted into ropes and walls of cabins are formed with black earth and alternate layers of heath, which also provides fuel in contact with good-quality burning peat; and we find that tobacco pipes are manufactured in France from the wood of the tree heath *arborea*, 'Brier' pipes as we call them, from the French word, 'bruyère'.

Heather as herbage for sheep, or grouse and other birds is referred to in Chapter II; and of the many other varied channels through which it has found an outlet for some common need, from a pigeon-cote roof to the sale of a sixpenny sprig in backing 'the winner' on the Derby race-course, the most intriguing is perhaps that of brewing beer.

It all began a very long time ago, when tradition asserts that a valuable recipe for manufacturing ale was known to the Danes—or it may have been the Picts! In any case, the last of one or the other, probably a Dane, was put to death for refusing to divulge the precious secret. To sacrifice one's life merely to safeguard a brew of beer seems a big price to pay. So the secret, which one day might have made a fortune for brewers—not that they are in need of it—is lost, and the beer with it.

Not to be outdone by the evil deed of the Picts, a much later generation in the island of Islay discovered their own concoction of heather ale, made from the ingredients of flowers, barley-malt, bog myrtle, tops of heather, hops and spices, aided by a little barm, the liquor being fermented with honey—a sort of floral shandy.

Some day, when in Scotland again, I must look in at Islay and order a pint of their stimulating beverage. If lucky enough to get one, I shall be luckier still to find a way back to England, and the Heather Garden.

CHAPTER XI

THE HEATHER CALENDAR

Stating the months during which the plants are in bloom

JANUARY

Erica carnea

alba – *carnea* – Cecilia M. Beale – Eileen Porter – *gracilis* – Mrs Sam Doncaster – *praecox rubra* – Queen Mary – Snow Queen – Winter Beauty.

Hybrids

darleyensis – George Rendall.

FEBRUARY

Erica carnea

alba – *carnea* – Cecilia M. Beale – Eileen Porter – *gracilis* – Loughrigg – Mrs Sam Doncaster – *praecox rubra* – Queen Mary – Springwood White – Springwood Pink – Snow Queen – Urville – *Vivellii* – Winter Beauty.

Hybrids

darleyensis – George Rendall.

MARCH

Erica carnea

alba – *atrorubra* – *carnea* – Cecilia M. Beale – C. J. Backhouse – Eileen Porter – *gracilis* – James Backhouse – King George – Loughrigg – Mrs Sam Doncaster – *pallida* – *praecox rubra* – Pink Pearl (or Pink Beauty) – Prince of Wales – Queen of Spain – Rosy Gem – Ruby Glow – Springwood White – Springwood Pink – Snow Queen – Thomas Kingscote – Urville – *Vivellii* – Winter Beauty.

Tree Heaths

arborea – *arborea alpina* – *arborea* Gold Tips – *australis* – *australis* Riverslea – *australis* Mr Robert – *canaliculata* – *lusitanica* (syn. *codonodes*) – *Veitchii*.

Erica mediterranea

alba – Brightness – *coccinea* – *hibernica* (syn. *glauca*) – *nana* – *rosea* – *rubra* – Silberschmeize – *superba* – W. T. Rackcliff.

Hybrids

darleyensis – George Rendall.

APRIL

Erica carnea

alba – *atrorubra* – *carnea* – C. J. Backhouse – Eileen Porter – James Backhouse – King George – Mrs Sam Doncaster – *pallida* – Pink Pearl (or Pink Beauty) – Prince of Wales – Queen of Spain – Rosy Gem – Ruby Glow – Springwood White – Springwood Pink – Thomas Kingscote.

Tree Heaths

arborea – *arborea alpina* – *arborea* Gold Tips – *australis* – *australis* Riverslea – *australis* Mr Robert – *canaliculata* – *lusitanica* (syn. *codonodes*) – *Veitchii*.

Erica mediterranea

alba – Brightness – *coccinea* – *hibernica* (syn. *glauca*) – *nana* – *rosea* – *rubra* – Silberschmeize – *superba* – W. T. Rackliff.

Erica umbellata

Hybrids

darleyensis – George Rendall.

MAY

Erica carnea

Some of the carneas are still flowering, even as late as mid-May; varieties such as: *pallida* – Pink Pearl (or Pink Beauty) – Prince of Wales – Queen of Spain – Rosy Gem – Ruby Glow – Thomas Kingscote.

Tree Heaths

arborea – *arborea alpina* – *arborea* Gold Tips – *australis* – *australis* Mr Robert – *australis* Riverslea – *canaliculata* – *lusitanica* (syn. *codonodes*) – *scoparia* – *Veitchii*.

Erica mediterranea

alba – Brightness – *coccinea* – *hibernica* (syn. *glauca*) – *rosea* – *rubra* – Silberschmeize – *superba* – W. T. Rackliff.

Erica umbellata

Daboëcia (Menziesia) polifolia

D. Azorica

JUNE

Erica mediterranea
rubra.

Erica cinerea
alba – alba major – alba minor – Apple Blossom – C. D. Eason – C. G. Best – *coccinea* – Domino – Eden Valley – Frances – Golden Drop – Golden Hue – G. Osmond – John Eason – *lilacina* – Mrs Dill – *pallida* – P. S. Patrick – *pygmaea* – *rosea* – Rose Queen – Rosabella – Ruby – Startler – *spicata* – *splendens* – *schizopetala* – Victoria.

Erica ciliaris
hybrida – *Maweana.*

Erica scoparia

Erica Tetralix
alba – *alba mollis* – Con. Underwood – L. E. Underwood – Mary Grace – Silver Bells.

Hybrids
Dawn – F. White – Gwavas – Gwen – H. Maxwell – *Stuartii* – W. G. Notley – Winifred Whiteley.

Daboëcia (Menziesia) polifolia
alba – *atropurpurea* – *bicolor* – *globosa.*
D. azorica

JULY

Erica cinerea
alba – *alba major* – *alba minor* – Apple Blossom – *atropurpurea* – *atrorubens* – *atrosanguinea* (Smith's variety) – *carnea* – C. D. Eason – *coccinea* – C. G. Best – Domino – Eden Valley – Frances – Golden Drop – Golden Hue – G. Osmond – John Eason – Knapp Hill variety – *lilacina* – Mrs Dill – *pallida* – P. S. Patrick – *purpurea* – *pygmaea* – *rosea* – Rose Queen – Rosabella – Ruby – Startler – *spicata* – *splendens* – *schizopetala* – Victoria.

Erica ciliaris
alba – *aurea* – *globosa* – *hybrida* – *Maweana* – Mrs C. H. Gill – *rotundifolia* – Stoborough – Wych.

Erica stricta

Erica Tetralix
alba – *alba mollis* – Con. Underwood – *darleyensis* – L. E. Under-

wood – *Lawsoniana* – *Mackaiana* – *Mackaiana plena* – Mary Grace – *praecox alba* – *Praegeri* – Pink Glow – *rubrum* – Ruby's variety – Silver Bells.

Hybrids
Dawn – F. White – Gwavas – Gwen – H. Maxwell – *Stuartii* – W. G. Notley – *Watsonii* – *Williamsiana* – Winifred Whiteley.

Daboëcia (Menziesia) polifolia
alba – atropurpurea – bicolor – globosa.

Calluna vulgaris
alba – Alportii praecox – aurea – dumosa - erecta – minor – pumila – tenuis.

AUGUST

Erica cinerea
alba – alba major – alba minor – Apple Blossom – *atropurpurea – atrorubens – atrosanguinea* (Smith's variety) – *carnea – coccinea –* Knapp Hill variety – *pallida – purpurea – rosea –* Rosabella.

Erica ciliaris
alba – aurea – globosa – hybrida – Maweana – Mrs C. H. Gill – *rotundifolia –* Stoborough – Wych.

Erica multiflora

Erica stricta

Erica Tetralix
alba – alba mollis – Con. Underwood – *Darleyensis –* L. E. Underwood – *Lawsoniana* – *Mackaiana* – *Mackaiana plena* – Mary Grace – *praecox alba* – *Praegeri* – Pink Glow – *rubrum* – Ruby's variety – Silver Bells.

Hybrids
Dawn – F. White – Gwavas – Gwen – H. Maxwell – *Stuartii* – W. G. Notley – *Watsonii* – *Williamsiana* – Winifred Whiteley.

Daboëcia (Menziesia) Polifolia
alba – atropurpurea – bicolor – globosa – Praegerae.

AUGUST AND SEPTEMBER

Erica cinerea
purpurea (September).

Erica ciliaris
globosa – *hybrida* – *Maweana* – Mrs C. H. Gill – *rotundifolia* – Stoborough – Wych.

Erica multiflora
Erica stricta
Erica Tetralix
alba mollis – Con. Underwood – L. E. Underwood – *Lawsoniana* – Mary Grace – *praecox alba* – *Praegeri* – *rubrum* – Ruby's variety – Silver Bells.

Erica vagans
alba – *carnea* – Cream – *grandiflora* – *kevernensis alba* – Lyonesse – Miss Waterer – Mrs D. F. Maxwell – *nana* – *pallida* – Pyrenees Pink – *rosea* – *rubra* – St Keverne.

Hybrids
Dawn – F. White – Gwavas – H. Maxwell – *Stuartii* – *Watsonii* – *Williamsiana*.

Daboëcia (Menziesia) polifolia
alba – *atropurpurea* – *bicolor* – *globosa* – *Praegerae*.

Calluna vulgaris
alba – *aurea* – August Beauty – *argentea* – *Alportii* – *Alportii praecox* – Carlton – Camla variety – *coccinea* – Cronix – County Wicklow – *cuprea* – C. W. Nix – *Darleyensis* – *dumosa* – *elata* (September) – *erecta* – *elegantissima* (white) – E. Hoare – *flore pleno* – *Foxii floribunda* – *Foxii nana* – *Grasmeriensis* – *Hammondii* – *Hammondii aurea* – *Hammondii rubrifolia* – *Hayesensis* – H. E. Beale – Hookstone – *hypnoides* – J. H. Hamilton – Kit Hill (September) – Kynance – Mair's variety – *minima* – *minor* – Mrs Pat – Mrs Ronald Gray – Mullion – *nana compacta* – *pallida* – *plena* – *pilosa* – *prostrata Kuphaldtii* – *pumila* – *pyramidalis* – *pygmaea* – *rigida* – Roma – *salmonoides* – *Searlei alba, rubra, aurea* (September) – Silver Queen – Sister Anne – *spicata* – *tenuis* – *tenella* – Tib – Tom Thumb – *tomentosa* (September) – *tricolorifolia* (Smith's variety) – *torulosa* – *Underwoodii*.

OCTOBER

Erica ciliaris
globosa – *Maweana* – Mrs C. H. Gill – *hybrida* – *rotundifolia* – Stoborough – Wych.

Erica Tetralix

alba mollis – Con. Underwood – Mary Grace – Ruby's variety – Silver Bells.

Erica vagans

alba – Cream – *kevernensis alba* – Lyonesse – Mrs D. F. Maxwell – *rubra*.

Hybrids

Dawn – F. White – Gwavas – Gwen – H. Maxwell – *Watsonii*.

Calluna vulgaris

David Eason – *elata* – *elegantissima* – *flore pleno* – Goldsworth Crimson – *hibernica* – *hyemalis* – Kit Hill – *Searlei alba* – *Searlei aurea* – *Searlei rubra* – *tomentosa* – *Underwoodii*.

NOVEMBER

Calluna vulgaris

David Eason – *elegantissima* – Goldsworth Crimson – *hibernica* – *hyemalis* – *Underwoodii*.

DECEMBER

Erica carnea

Eileen Porter – *gracilis* – Queen Mary – Winter Beauty.

Calluna vulgaris

elegantissima – *hyemalis*.

INDEX

The figures in black type indicate main references. Figures in brackets indicate illustrations.